WELCOME TO
NEW LONDON

WELCOME TO
NEW LONDON

Journeys and encounters in the
post-Olympic city

JOHN ROGERS

Jacket design: Patrick Knowles
Photographs by John Rogers

Published by:
the lost byway
7 Bell Yard, London, WC2A 2JR
www.thelostbyway.com

British Library Cataloguing-in-Publication Data.
A catalogue record for this book is available from
the British Library

ISBN: 978-1-7395392-0-7
First edition: 2023

CONTENTS

INTRODUCTION

One sunny midweek afternoon in late May 2023 I accepted an invitation from audio recordist Joel Carr to take a wander through the shifting sounds of London. We decided to start this sonic perambulation at Chrisp Street Market in Poplar. The market had been created as a key component of the Lansbury Estate which was presented in the 1951 Festival of Britain as a new model urban neighbourhood. The Lansbury and Chrisp Street were part of an exhibition of 'live architecture'. Fostering and nurturing 'the identity of existing communities' was at the very heart of the scheme and captured the mood of post-war rebuilding. In 2023 it was now the subject of a £300 million regeneration project.

We made our way from Langdon Park DLR Station with the towers of Canary Wharf framing the skyline ahead. Chrisp Street itself, which had been the site of the original Victorian costermongers' market, had gained colourful panelled hoardings boasting of the benefits of the coming regeneration. We turned off the street past a beleaguered looking pub on the corner of the market square.

Chalked on the out-side blackboard the menu offered quarter pounder burgers for £2, and Sunday roasts for £7.

The market traders were beginning to pack away their wares, which was the reason Joel chose this time of day to record the sounds of the final sales pitches and the clanking metal struts of the market stalls. The sun threw angular de Chirico shadows across the square, something I imagined the architect Frederick Gibberd had intricately planned when he designed this as Britain's 'first purpose-built pedestrian shopping area'. At the time this was a vaunted scheme, showcasing an optimistic vision of the world that could rise from the bombsites. Gibberd's design was copied in towns and cities across the land. The regeneration project planned to radically reshape the market area retaining just a few of the Festival of Britain buildings. Would Joel's soundscape and the images I captured on camera become part of an archive of the disappeared? As we made our way through the market towards the Limehouse Cut I experienced a moment of panic that Chrisp Street and Poplar was yet another zone of transition not included in this book.

When I'd started writing in the summer of 2013 the aim had been relatively simple: to document a new London that was emerging from the ashes of the Olympic flames. My previous book, This Other London had been inspired by topographical writers of the early twentieth century who'd explored the new London given birth by the expansion of the railways and had seen suburbs sprout in the fields around the city. My walks in overlooked London were a rediscovery of their territory. So now I felt I had a duty to do the same in this century as nascent villages and suburbs were once again spawning across the capital.

Writing in 1947 Harold P. Clunn observed in London Marches On: 'To produce a book on London absolutely up-to-date, even though no new buildings were erected for several years, is uncommonly like attempting to emulate the feat of Joshua who commanded the sun to stand still'. And so that has been the case. I've had to accept that there are many important stories about contemporary London not included in this book. For example, the massive and contested redevelopment of Elephant and Castle which saw the deletion of the Heygate Estate. Barking Riverside also didn't make it into these pages despite two visits with my camera stalking out the terrain. I intended to write about the inspiring story of how the tenants on Leathermarket Estate in Borough built a block of council-owned flats in the very shadow of the Shard. But that remains as a chapter in a documentary I made with the tenants' associations of the area. That's aside from all the solo walks around the capital I documented on my YouTube channel. During the lockdowns of 2020-2021 connecting with the hyperlocal and peeling back the layers of every tree and stretch of tarmac became more essential than ever to my wellbeing. People shared wonderful recollections and anecdotes in the comments on YouTube. Precious nuggets of social history were dropped on those pages by viewers around the world (and still are). It was a reminder of the strength of the bond we form with the everyday environments around us.

After my first deliberate post-Olympic circuit of Stratford in 2013, my wife warned me this would be a 10-year project. It turned out that she was right. The story kept shifting and moving, and I had to keep following it.

The book starts in 2013 as the Olympic village in Stratford transitioned to become a new permanent settlement, and the Stratford City plan became a reality. My early mapping of this terrain triggered a series of encounters with brilliant people and communities that came to define the journey that unfolded. This was a narrative that I strongly believed needed to be captured, an important moment in the ever-evolving story of London.

This trail was not just a reportage of present events, but it unexpectedly led me into the deep past, as one encounter led to another – from the Carpenters Estate in Stratford to the campaign to Save Soho and a chance conversation with a Pearly Punk King on the rooftop of the old Foyles building which took me through Epping Forest to the prehistory of London in the upper Lea Valley. And then somehow the United Nations sent me to Peckham.

Most of the events recorded here took place between 2013 and 2016 but have been updated where possible until the last moment before publication. It has truly been an enlightening journey. The map is the characters. The story is of the power of place and community and the eternal resilience of this incredible city.

CHAPTER 1

THE EAST VILLAGE

A year after the 2012 Olympic Games the Queen Elizabeth Olympic Park was still hidden behind a wrapper of steel mesh fencing. Sounds of Bruce Springsteen and the E Street Band's gig at the Olympic Stadium had wafted east over the rooftops to where I lay under the sumac tree in my garden two-and-a-half-miles away in Leytonstone. But otherwise, E20 remained an enigma to me. An angry tweet I sent from the excuse of a pub that dangled off the end of Westfield Stratford City like an aggravated haemorrhoid was about to change that. I'd seen the cuboid display showing off the development of E20 on one of the outdoor concourses of Westfield. E20 was a postcode that had previously only existed in the gritty fictional soap opera world of East Enders and then been conjured into a kind of reality. A reality that the glossy PR presented as being a world away from the trials of Pauline Fowler and the chain-smoking Dot Cotton.

The Cow at Westfield had all the charm and authenticity of an airport bar. There was an over-predominance of men in pastel

1

shirts with the collars turned up. I sat there pondering how E20 completely messed with the alphabetical London postcode system which, after attributing the number 1 to the principal district post office, follows alphabetically, hence E2 is Bethnal Green, E3 is Bow, and E4 way out east in Chingford – there is no E19, and East Village doesn't follow Woodford / South Woodford in the alphabet (and you couldn't get round this by calling it Olympic Park either). I worried that this could present a serious threat to the numerical matrix that holds London together – the mystical numerological system that binds the oscillating suburbs into a material whole and stops them flying off into the gravitational field of the surrounding counties. With the arrival of East Village E20, Wanstead could end up back in Essex, Woolwich in Kent, Wimbledon in Surrey, Wood Green in Hertfordshire. The entire county of Middlesex could re-emerge overnight to swallow West London whole. It would be like the ravens deserting the Tower of London, or when Johnny Marr quit The Smiths – seemingly impregnable empires crumble.

I decided to take action and did what any angry middle-aged man in a pub would do. I sent the first tweet to the East Village account:

'@EastVillageLDN London is a great ancient city – so why have you borrowed a name associated with New York? Very disappointing.'

I took another swig of beer and thought that I hadn't fully captured my ire so I followed up with another:

'Insulting. London's newest suburb took its name from an area of New York @EastVillageLDN says lot bout their respect for this grt ancient city.'

2

That was more like it.

After venting my spleen in 140 characters on a social network I drank the rest of my pint and crunched through the over-priced crisps and went home, unnerved by the new London in the glass case and the numerical Armageddon it was about to unleash.

Next morning I woke up to an unexpected reply on Twitter from East Village London:

'@fugueur Hi John, we're sorry you feel that way. Please DM us your details & I can send over some info regarding our name choice.'

The Twitter exchange ended up in an invitation to tour the East Village site with a group of bloggers. The charm offensive was in full swing, I was being PR-ed, presented with a unique opportunity to get a look around 'London's newest neighbourhood' in its nascent form before a single resident had moved in. We were the future opposition being buttered up and co-opted in advance. The charming young man in the PR office confessed to me via email that he'd never been to the real East Village – 'You'd like it', I told him, 'there's a great comic book store as I remember. Will there be a comic book store in your East Village?' 'Er, I'm not sure, I doubt it to be honest', he admitted.

We were to rendezvous near one of the food courts of Westfield Stratford City. This vast retail colony covered 1.9 million square feet and was built on a former locative building works that had been active since the 1840s. The shopping mall made the bold claim of being 'a new metropolitan capital for East London, a city within a city'. The explosion of noise entering Westfield was something I'll never get used to. There were people laid out on massage chairs outside the toilets being electronically wobbled so the blubber around their jowls vibrated and the loose change in their pockets rattled like metal maracas. The whole scene was bizarre. The wide gleaming corridor leading down to the RV point stank of sewage – despite the swanky façade there were clearly problems with the drains. A young man escorting two ladies pulling wheelie suitcases out of Stratford International announced 'The largest urban shopping centre in Europe'. A woman led a guided tour along the main concourse – retail tourists. There was the atmosphere of a desert outpost – a Dubai development.

There were two other bloggers on the tour and we spotted each other instantly. One was an editor from the excellent Londonist blog, the other the eponymous author of a popular personal blog who'd posted a couple of pithy comments on my links on Reddit in the past. I decided not to bring this up – maybe an opportunity would present itself later on the tour. We chatted about Crossrail about which I knew very little except for the odd archaeological find, not engaging with it as a piece of transport infrastructure but as a giant multi-billion pound archaeological dig.

The charming young man from the press team who answered my tweet arrived followed by a couple of clipboard-toting hardened PR types who eyed us suspiciously. We were then led through a series of turnstiles to a portacabin to get togged up in protective boots, hard hats, high-vis vests and goggles before being met by the fella who'd be leading the tour, a construction professional. His manner instantly conveyed that he was a person who dealt in facts, bricks, cinder blocks, quantities of sand and cement, and logistics – a man who got things done. I was keen to see at some point how he might react to some of my almost spiritual laments towards his creation.

First stop was the wetlands area, where we were told that the water gathered in the ponds was used to irrigate the parkland and flush the toilets in the East Village flats. Fish larvae had already found their way into the pond transported on the feet of visiting birds. The first permanent residents had arrived.

An area of vertical deadwood had been created to provide a habitat for stag beetles. There were bat and bird boxes, a sand martin hotel, and an otter holt. I pointed out that nesting otters had been spotted in the Lea the evening before building work on the Olympic development had started: otters being easily unsettled they would have soon fled further upriver to safety. They conceded no otters had been sighted although kingfishers had been seen and a peregrine falcon dropped in for fresh vermin. A crow cawed loudly over the scrunching of our feet on the new gravel path. We crossed Olympic Park Avenue to Portlands, another of the landscaped areas that the PR people were keen to trumpet. But as it was the naming of this new settlement that had brought me there I asked why it was called Portlands. They didn't know. I took a plunge into the unknown and hazarded that it was an association with the portland stone used to build many of the grand buildings across London including St Paul's, the British Museum and Buckingham Palace, quarried from the town of Portland in Dorset. They looked back blankly.

The site was formed from the tunnellings of the Channel Tunnel rail link, soil fresh from the underbelly of Stratford, clean of invasive weeds and plants. Three types of meadow mixtures were sown into the soft landscaping – damp meadow, dry, and woodland beneath the trees. The streets leading off Portlands, Scarlet Close and Logan Close, took their names from the red and blue Olympic rings (Logan sapphires and blue loganberries). The scarlet / red theme was then extended to the naming of a series of housing blocks designed by Denton Corker Marshall. Sienna from the natural pigment found in cave paintings and named after the Tuscan city where it was used during the Renaissance. Venetian House after another earth pigment coloured by iron oxide again favoured by Italian artists of the Renaissance. It took quite a leap of the imagination to conjure up the burnt umber earth of Tuscan hills and resplendent Venetian frescos stood there looking at the empty blank slabs. Amelia Mansions takes its name from a variety of strawberry. They could have continued the Italian Renaissance theme as there's a variety of strawberry called Florence. Zinnia Mansions from the red Mexican flower discovered by the 18th century German botanist Johann Gottfried Zinn. Sable House for the berry of that name (it's also those lovely biscuits with the jam love heart in the middle). Torero Mansions is more difficult to decipher but appears to have some relationship to bullfighting so maybe it's the red cape that lures the enraged bull to its doom. The information from the Press Release was decidedly thin so I'm making these extended links from a single word in brackets eg strawberry, colour, for Terero it says 'red route'. Titian Mansions and Sedona House are from red varieties of roses. Titian though is more likely to make you think of the Venetian artist. It's a shame they didn't have the courage to paint the blocks in the colours of their names (Titian would have): the changing hues of the vertical colour chart as the glorious Lea Valley sunset did its daily flypast would have been one of the great sights of the city.

The editor from Londonist asked if people would know which athletes had lived in each flat – would you know if it had been Usain Bolt's pad, imagining his great legs dangling off the end of the too-short beds? The PR man replied that tenants wouldn't know, that however good it was to celebrate the Olympians who were here before, it was a new community. At the time I believed the echo of its former life as the Olympic Athletes' Village would always be there, included on some obscure tourist trail, a living relic of the London 2012 Games. I'm not entirely sure that has held true. It seems to be better known for its proximity to Westfield.

Although the flats looked new, they were not, like those refurbished electrical goods you get on the cheap because someone opened the box and sent them back. New but used at the same time. At this stage London's newest neighbourhood was empty, the apartments in the process of having kitchens added as cooking facilities were a necessary sacrifice to squeeze 22,000 athletes into a development that once converted would house between 8-9,000 residents.

We stood outside the block where the British athletes had lived. I suggested it would have been a big advantage during the Games not to have lived here. The Building Man cut me a dirty look and hastily moved on to point out the quality of materials used in the park. Twelve or thirteen thousand square metres of York stone all from the same supplier in Halifax, carefully chosen with a huge amount of care. One hundred and eighty London plane trees planted throughout the park, the signature tree of the city, the biggest ready-grown trees you can get. It was imagined their leaf canopies would join hands across the walkways. The trees were reflected in a sculptural labyrinth of polished steel created by Danish artist Jeppe Hein. There were fears that this could confuse birdlife. A study was carried out which concluded that the birds could distinguish between a tree and a reflection of a tree.

We'd had environmentalism, art and the ghosts of Olympic greats but I wanted to know who owned it all. They attempted to fudge an answer by saying that the roads will pass under the control of Newham council with the rest falling under an estate management company. 'Is it private?' I persisted. 'It's not a gated community', the PR insisted. They were clearly on the defensive against the fears that East Village would become an enclave of privilege in one of the most deprived areas of London.

East Village is co-owned by Triatholon Homes, an affordable housing organisation, and Get Living, 'a partnership between Qatari Diar, wholly owned by the Qatar Investment Authority, and clients of Delancey, a specialist real estate investment and advisory company'. Qatar Investment Authority is the investment fund for the Qatari government with all those billions of petrodollars to spend, in this case on the prime real estate produced by the 'Green Olympics'. They most famously bought Paris St Germain football club but also held shares in Barclays Bank, a large chunk of Sainsburys, Shell, Canary Wharf, Heathrow, and splashed out £1.5 billion on Harrods.

It's just as well they weren't involved in the construction of the site when you read the horror stories of the conditions for workers building the facilities for the 2022 World Cup in Qatar. According to an article in the Guardian, Nepalese workers were dying at a rate of one each day during the summer in 2013, and another Guardian report estimated that up to 6500 migrant workers had died in Qatar in the 10 years leading up to the 2022 World Cup. Working conditions, they said, amounted to a form of 'modern day slavery'.

The focus of the tour though wasn't on ownership or human rights but landscaping and ecology. Scots pines had been planted at great expense to bring a bit of Epping Forest back into the heart of East London. Landforms were created to produce hidden views and an air of mystery. Some thought had been given to attempting to design some kind of 'soul' from the flat earth. That, I was informed, lay behind the use of 'Village' in the name – a referencing of the Athletes' Village and the village atmosphere they hoped to create with the school, medical centre, housing and independent shops around a green space. Once the fences came down and the kids started traipsing into the school built to service the development, it was believed the wider community would start to filter through. They were keen to point out that the Athletes' Village was only half of the whole development, the rest was still to be built, continuing to evolve over time. London's newest neighbourhood, at this point still sheathed in hoardings and aluminium fencing with hard-hat construction workers trundling around on plant machinery, had another future awaiting before it had even come to life. Its place in the spotlight was short-lived as the more upmarket Chobham Manor and International Quarter rose around its borders, then new blocks filled in the gaps, slowly blotting out the sunlight. What we were looking at in that first post-Olympic summer, was a half-built Lego set.

The tour ended and the other bloggers headed off for a pint at Tap East in the Westfield food court with its beers brewed on the premises – a tempting option on a boiling day. But my tour wasn't over. I wanted to survey the wider site, to find the limits of the new Stratford. I skirted the edge of Westfield Stratford City, a concept that seemed to emerge from the Stratford City Challenge in the early 1990s. The City Challenge was a government scheme devised to regenerate deprived inner-city areas and reverse what was seen as urban decline partly through private sector property development backed by central government support. The Stratford bid claimed that its 'vision' was 'to put the heart back into East London. We will make Stratford a commercial magnet, looking to Europe and on to the millennium with a vibrant shopping centre, new secure housing and a wealth of arts, entertainment and culture reflecting the diversity of East London's communities. It will become the focus of East London's regeneration.'

Looking at Stratford City from the raised hump in the road having passed around and through its tubes, pipes and blow holes it terrified me. In its base form my reaction was fear, but where did that fear come from? The hulk of the development seemed so alien and out of place. An attempt to over-write the past, forget Stratford of the 20th century, or Stratford-atte-Bowe of the Middle Ages with Queen Maud nearly drowning in the feisty waters of the Lea, forget the Stratford mocked by Chaucer. Stratford City was loaded with American resonances: Atlantic City, Kansas City, Oklahoma City, Gotham City.

But it was another American city that was the generator of my ill-ease. A fictional future made manifest here in East London – Mega City One, the future dystopia policed by Judge Dredd, a world I filled my head with every week in the pages of the comic 2000 AD. When my Dad came on home from work on Fridays with our order from the newsagent I would rush upstairs and devour it in one sitting lying on my bed. It was a dark world of violent 'Block Manias' where residents of super high-rises would go to war against each other, hyper-obese people who have wheels attached to their enormous sagging guts, radioactive genetic mutations, and post-nuclear wastelands beyond the Mega City walls. And now its shadow loomed across the place I called home.

The view from the flyover into the park cast north across the Orbit sculpture, the Aquatics Centre and the stadium. The disturbed earth of this transitionary stage before the flanks of the Aquatics Centre became a grassy bank offered a brief hint of the distant past, the first residents of the Olympic Park. Archaeological excavations uncovered a middle Bronze Age settlement of roundhouses within an embankment lying beside a worked field system. Just beyond the settlement, two skeletons were unearthed buried in a crouched position, both male, one with noteworthy wear to his teeth that was deemed to extend beyond merely poor dental hygiene, as if his teeth had been systematically worn down. He also had a dodgy left knee, something that I could easily relate to, imagining an archaeologist puzzling over my heap of bones in 3000 years trying to unravel the mystery of the bevelled contours of my left knee worn into jagged shards by repeated urban wanderings.

The settlement was of a relatively rare 'Springfield-style enclosure', indicating that this may have been a significant point within the region around 1400 BC. Another similar 'Springfield' settlement was found in Oliver Close, Leyton, a short distance away,

10

most likely linked in some way. A loom weight was excavated, a whole antler placed within a pit, and animal bone fragments from sheep, goats, pigs, and dwarf cattle. John Payne concluded in his article about the site in London Archaeologist that 'One could hypothesise a situation where the Aquatics Centre site acted as a focus for the people who harvested wild flora and fauna from the adjacent areas of marshland'.

East Village was also occupied in the same period. Six cremation burials were uncovered in the area around Stratford International and the Wetlands where we'd been led on the tour, the prehistory of the development not meriting a single mention from our guides, not even when we stood where the burial urns had been dug up or when we walked over the footprints of the roundhouses, now tarmacked over. This was clearly an area of activity from at least the middle Bronze Age, a focal point within the nascent London region, taking advantage of the fertile marshlands.

The Bronze Age is considered to be the era that saw the birth of urban civilisation, with the spread of metalworking and forms of writing. Payne pointed out the historical symmetry between the early Stratford village and the first Olympics in Greece, calling it the 'first Olympic Village'. It was established in the same period as the Trojan Wars, when Brutus, according to one of London's foundation myths, would have fled to this mysterious Isle of the Dead shrouded in the mists of the Channel to build his citadel. It raises the possibility that this could have been an eastern outpost of Brutus's 'New Troy'.

Evidence was found of occupation expanding on the site in the Iron Age with further roundhouses, continuing through the Romano-British period with discoveries of more burials and shards of Samian pottery, blood red like the names of the blocks in East Village. Looking out from the bridge, even with a squint it was hard to conjure that pre-Roman landscape back into existence. What we see today has been warped by the multiple layers of made ground dumped by the industrial period. But until the 19th century, this was a rural terrain, worked agricultural land for thousands of years subject to the seasonal flooding of the Lea and the frayed watery tendrils that branch off the main root as it passes through Stratford into Bow forming the Bow Back Rivers. Folklore suggested that some of these watercourses were created by the armies of Alfred the Great to strand a Viking fleet that had sailed up the Lea. A Viking longboat recovered from the mud on Tottenham Marshes lends weight to the story. Older watercourses were also found by the archaeological digs, it was not only bones, beads and broken pots that are dug up but rivers. The Tumbling Bay Stream wound its way across the marshes as did a nameless tributary that ran near the Aquatics Centre where the waters of the Lea and the Waterworks River still flow. Before work started on the Olympic Park nature was in the process of reclaiming the land and reversing the tide of history, buddleia, willowherb, and knotweed subsuming the piles of discarded junk. Left to its own devices this would have become a resplendent urban wilderness. For all the talk on the tour of the ecological credentials of East Village the most environmentally consistent thing to do would be not to move thousands of people and businesses into the area. But that wasn't an option, the industrial blight of the previous 150 years was used as the benchmark, erasing the tens of thousands of years that preceded it.

The old Roman road from the port of London to Camulodunum (Colchester) passed through Stratford here, near where the DLR scuttles along to Canary Wharf and down to Lewisham. The road I was standing on harked back to a later invasion – Montfichet Road is named after the Norman Baron who claimed the estates of the Saxon freemen Leured and Alestan acquiring the Barony of Ham. One of the great antiquarians of East and West Ham, a cricket-loving Prussian immigrant called Dr Pagenstecher, wrote a wonderful flowing narrative history of East and West Ham published in 1908. On the period of the Norman Conquest he noted 'Thus landed property was wrested from its native holders and bestowed on foreign chieftains'. Looking south over the rooftops of Carpenters Estate, the vista was punctured with the new tower blocks branded as 'luxury apartments', which has become such an overworn phrase I'm already vowing to avoid its use again. This was the landscape where the next battles would be fought over the future of Stratford, and to a degree the future of London. There was a landgrab going on, with the Olympics a success and the TV coverage showing aerial shots of all the vacant brownfield sites lining the Lea Valley and the Royal Docks – an advert for the development potential for this end of the East. I heard Ken Livingstone eagerly boast of how for him as Mayor of London at the time, the Olympics was a way to sell East London to the investors of the dynamic growing economies of China, Brazil and India. The Qatari Royal Family were just the first to get on board.

Moving down Montfichet Road (which apparently should be pronounced 'Mon-fish-A' although to do so round these parts would make you sound like the worst kind of Hyacinth Bucket / Abigail's Party snob, so I preferred it with a hard spitting T on the end) and beneath the railway bridge I somehow managed to achieve the impossible and find myself on the wrong side of a roundabout. A cable dangled down from the tracks looped into a noose – an ill omen. This was the new Stratford half-formed, its fate had been decided but the cash hadn't quite yet been scraped together to finish the job, like a half-built extension on a suburban semi.

The Icona residential block with its colourful translucent balconies was seemingly inspired by a packet of the iconic '70s boiled sweets, a giant model of a packet of Spangles with the wrapper removed and stood on end. Across the street it fronted it out with a brownbrick office building, all smashed windows like a toothless old bareknuckle bruiser who's had one fight too many but refuses to lie down. Even the urban explorers didn't bother to venture inside.

A kid kicked a ball around on the corner of Biggerstaff Road on the edge of Carpenters Estate, the awkward left-over of the indigenous community who refused to be uprooted, the estate that refused to die.

I turned up Bridgewater Road facing the early evening sun and over a bridge that spans the Waterworks River. Yellow plastic stoppers had been placed over the spikes that top the railing with gaffer-taped remains of mesh flapping in the breeze. There was something almost tribal about it, a warning not to enter hostile lands. But, there was a green sign marked 'Pedestrian Route', and I've spent time with headhunters in Borneo so nothing was keeping

14

me out. The signage was either overly optimistic or deliberately misleading because 20 yards later the path led straight into a pen of metal fencing which was apparently there to protect a patch of purple loosestrife.

I followed the banks of the City Mill River, the air full of a pungent riverine aroma. Seagulls whirled overhead. I wished I had a kayak after discovering the joy of paddling on the Regent's Canal that summer. An old fella unfolded his chair and cast off into the water. 'Going to catch much?' I asked. 'Used to', he says, 'but haven't been for years, don't expect much but gives me something to do'. Unlike the frantic cycle commuters on the Regent's Canal, these towpaths were deserted. The Lock Keeper's Cottage, painted brilliant blue, had weeds climbing out of the cracks around the foundations reaching high up the walls.

A large flock of cackling seagulls mustered over Marshgate Lane. This area should have a heritage listing to show what the rest of the park was like till the Olympic Games, with people subsidised to carry on working in the light Industrial units as a demonstration of 20th century life in the lower Lea Valley before it was totally transformed into an amenity zone. This was a change that had been on the cards for a while – earmarked in the County of London Plan drawn up in 1943. The population of the area more than halved during the war due to the intense bombing of the docks and the eastern industrial belt and never fully recovered. Around 51,000 homes in West Ham and Stratford were destroyed by bombing and much of the remaining buildings incurred some sort of damage. An area that had been one of the biggest and most productive industrial centres in Britain at the beginning of the 20th century came bottom of a national league table of socio-economic deprivation in the early '90s when Stratford became one of Michael Heseltine's City Challenges.

The industrial heritage of the area stretched back more than 1000 years. The Domesday Book listed eight mills around this section of the river alone. The mills persisted right up until the railways moved in and brought gasworks and chemical plants. Household names such as Bryant and May and Yardley moved in – both sites now residential. An entire way of life had gone from this part of East London. It was easy to see the relationship between the rows of terraced housing that spilt out of the railways and the docks, but these new empty units are the work of unseen forces: they can't all be working the kiosks in the Olympic Park and have jobs in Sports Direct (even though Stratford has two branches). It baffled and unnerved me. My instinct was to keep moving, more so than when I used to walk home through here in the early hours of the morning on my way back from the City Poly Student Union Bar in Aldgate to my room in Forest Gate in those deprived times of the late '80s and early '90s.

On the other side of Stratford High Street, further development will transform the area around Sugar Mill Lane with the building of 1200 residential units (of which only a tiny proportion appeared to be 'affordable'), shops, offices and a hotel. Most alarming of all it was being built by IKEA (or at least a company associated enough with IKEA for the press to dub it 'IKEA city'). I take a deep breath and cross my fingers every time I place a book on my IKEA bookshelf and I'd need some convincing to crawl through the door of an IKEA Wendy House so can't begin to understand who would dare to dwell in a block of IKEA flats. Would residents get an allen key with the deeds? The building of a giant wicker Olympic torch hardly instilled confidence.

The transformation of this zone will be so complete that it may only survive in the memories of the people who lived and worked here before Olympic Year Zero, like the signwriters I met one evening when I was invited to screen my documentary about the artist Bob and Roberta Smith in an old factory. They'd come along as Bob utilises signwriting in his vivid text paintings and sculptures.

16

The factory that had been converted into a temporary cinema had been the signwriting workshop where they'd worked. Films shot around the area have already become heritage artefacts – Bronco Bullfrog, a cult classic, will become as important as the Dead Sea Scrolls. Sparrers Can't Sing from 1963 was based on a play devised by Joan Littlewood at Stratford's Theatre Royal and shows residents moving into the new tower blocks that now look the worse for wear next to the gleaming erections going up all around, which in turn will seem shabby in 50 years. Deep End will be watched in slow-motion picking out the dark night streets of industrial Stratford. Even the recent films by Paul Kelly, the brilliantly titled What Have You Done Today Mervyn Day (2005), and Seven Summers already seem obscure with vistas difficult to place.

Bow Flyover was a line in the sand that I wouldn't cross on this trek, respecting the old tribal, and later administrative boundaries.

To the west of here had been the domain of London County Council, the eastern folk were country bumpkins. Hackney people saw moving to Leytonstone as relocating to the countryside: some still do evidenced by the way they bowl around E11 in their wax jackets and wellies. I needed to complete a loop around the Olympic Park to try and get it into my head, to attempt some sort of understanding of what monster was spawning on the marshes.

I headed up the Lea to the Hackney Cut being buzzed by cyclists. A bargeful of hipsters glided past. A small community of houseboat dwellers lived in the shadow of the Olympic Stadium. Looking across at the bulbous apartment building bullying the Lea I couldn't even raise a single drop of bile: I was apparently suffering anti-gentrification fatigue. They'd beaten me and I hadn't even completed my inaugural journey of the quest. Hackney Wick on the far bank was too much to take in on this tour, I'd been shredded by the Stratford experience.

I broke my stride for the first time since leaving home by stopping at the Crate brewery bar on the banks of the water. Over the way, teams were busy removing the accumulated graffiti of decades and replacing it with officially sanctioned street art. There was something brutal about this destruction of spontaneous culture, an erasure of local heritage: some of the pieces were far more than hastily sprayed tags, more like huge elaborate murals. The blank spaces between the commissioned works were coated with a substance that prevented the unofficial artists from adding their mark.

Refreshed I pushed on, fuelled by the determination to complete the circuit. The canal was thick with green chickweed. White trumpets of bindweed heralded the turn towards Leyton along the old forest road. In 1724 Daniel Defoe wrote of the discovery of a stone causeway believed to be the remnants of another Roman road into Essex, 'That the great road lay this way and that the great causeway landed again just over the river, where now the Temple-mills stand, and passed by Sir Tho. Hick's house at Ruckolls (Ruckholts), all this is not doubted; and that it was one of those famous highways made by the Romans, there is undoubted proof, by the several marks of Roman work and by Roman coins, and other antiquities found there'. Defoe also mentions the steep increase in rents in Stratford and the other villages bordering the Lea and the construction of a thousand new houses 'since the Revolution ... being chiefly for the habitation of the richest citizens, such as either are able to keep two houses, one in the country and one in the City'.

The setting sun lit a golden path down the Lea, a runway laid out for the gods to return to earth and do a bit of late-night shopping at Westfield and feast at the Chicago Ribshack in the food court. If you follow the idea that human life was deliberately seeded on earth by extra-terrestrials with the secret encoded within our DNA, I'm fairly certain the purpose wasn't to build shopping malls. If life is just one giant alien experiment this is the point the ETs might conclude it had all been a colossal waste of time and effort – seven million years of evolution to produce Stratford City.

Performing their routine flyover surveys, our alien creators would have seen the way the Bronze Age inhabitants sought out a suitable gravel island between the clear flowing watercourses to place their encampment, watching it grow slowly over hundreds of years from two communal dwellings to eight or nine between the Lea and Leyton. Then with horror, they would have witnessed how the same generation who decoded the human genome decided to smash mother nature to bits, lacquer her in concrete and place more than 20,000 people where only recently within the context of human history had lived less than 100. Let's hope the Alien Creator theory is wrong for this reason alone.

What we do know is that in The Book of Boris, Johnson's '2020 Vision for London', the development and rebuilding of Stratford was an integral part of his new Brand London, overtly stating how the TV images from the Games gave the city a 'positive glow' and directly led to 'billions of pounds of international investment'. Chobham Manor, East Wick, Sweetwater, Stratford Waterfront, Pudding Mill, and the International Quarter were all at various stages of construction within the area of my circuit between that initial walk and the publication of this book. The Mayor also unveiled plans for a new cultural hub in the Queen Elizabeth Park, dubbing it with the near unpronounceable moniker 'Olympicopolis', featuring offshoots of the V&A, Sadler's Wells and even a transatlantic annex of the Smithsonian (this was thankfully rebranded East Bank).

They had a model on display in a vacant shop in Westfield showing East Village complete with coloured details of windows, balconies and trees. Around it loomed featureless white monolithic forms of the buildings in the pipeline surrounding the site. By comparison East Village appeared as a Hobbit shire beside this other spectral city.

My walk ended as I passed Leyton spelt out in large metallic letters on sticks planted in the soil of the old mills owned by the Knights Templar. Any mention of the Templars gets the pulses racing for the lovers of a good yarn, raising hopes of buried Biblical secrets, the proof that Jesus was a Druid who converted to our island faith on his tin-buying visits to Cornwall with Joseph of Arimathea. That kind of thing anyway. However, in reality, the Templars owned so much land and property that it's akin to celebrating the site of a branch of KFC hoping to find the Colonel's secret recipe buried in the basement.

This slice of Templar land beneath the bird-box sign remained undeveloped. Down there in the undergrowth, the Dagenham Brook slid beneath the Temple Mills railway sidings to make its confluence with the River Lea. Leytonstone's lost Philley Brook mysteriously vanished into the earth here also. The ruins of Ruckholts House held onto their secrets. A fabulous tale had been spun from this corner of East London which had been passed on to me via email.

The email was a treasury of local folklore and recounted an exchange between two old allotment holders who held plots in the area. It started off prosaically, pondering the question of flooding in the area and the locations of potential lost underground streams. They recounted the story of how plans for the Victorian local sewage and drainage system were lost in a dispute between two brothers and ended up being fed to a goat and lost to history. Ruckholt, this curious correspondence claimed, is derived from Rock Halt and was formed of a dry piece of high land in the marshes which had been fortified by a Viking who used it as a stronghold from which to dominate this section of the marshes.

The streams running through these marshes, they said, were mentioned by Julius Caesar in an account of suppressing a rebellion at Ilford. And indeed there was a Roman villa on the course of one of the streams and also some intriguing recently-discovered Roman roads through Leyton. These streams fed a pond known as Jesus Christ's Cup, due to its constant pure running water. A hermit named Cedric dwelt beside this 'magical spring' for a while.

And King Harold may even have watered his horses here on his way to Waltham Abbey. The watercourses fed watercress beds which were tended by the Leyton marshmen and boatmen. When Jospeh Bazalgette constructed his sewer system for London in the 1860s, sewage works were built here on the marshes. The destruction of the watercress beds enraged the marshmen so much that a great battle took place involving the army deploying muskets and swords resulting in much loss of life. Reporting of the outrage was suppressed for fear of sparking a general uprising. A much older allotment holder passed on the story of seeing his father's 'cutlass slash' down his face that he'd earned at the great battle of Leyton marshes. It's such a magnificent story that I want every word of it to be true.

CHAPTER 2

THE SECOND CIRCUIT

This first circuit hadn't been enough to begin my understanding of London's newest neighbourhood. I mentioned it to Chris, the father of one of the mums I knew from the school run (the networks formed in the school playground are the most powerful I've ever come across). Chris had lived on Clays Lane Estate, once the biggest tenant-owned housing co-op in Europe which had the misfortune of being situated on what would become the Olympic site. Chris offered to take me on his own orbital tour of the area.

Here I was on a hot Thursday afternoon in July 2013, the temperature pushing upwards in the direction of 30 degrees. The Shard shimmered at the end of my road seven miles away in the distance. Whatever message The Shard had intended to convey to the citizenry of London had been hijacked first by a group of fearless urban explorers who had clambered to its summit before it was finished, and then by intrepid Greenpeace protestors who decorated it with a banner which read 'Save the Arctic'. The Shard was now a peak to be conquered like Everest or Kilimanjaro.

The entry point to my own quest would not involve crampons and ropes – I suffer from mild vertigo – but a quick left-turn into a parallel street that I rarely walked down. This simple manoeuvre kickstarted a process of defamiliarisation as suddenly I was in a territory of unknown privet hedges. Unlike the adjacent street where I live, this one has distinctive wooden awnings over the front doors with carved trim and stained glass mosaics of imagined utopias featuring sunrise lands of green hills and valleys – the delicate finesses of Edwardian house builders. These small details made it alien enough to feel like another realm – a different sensibility to the builders who erected my street with its black and white diamond-tiled front paths and cream and green paintwork that many houses still sported.

These Leytonstone streets rose from farmland in a swift burst of 20 years between the end of the 19th century and the start of the 20th. London was breaking out – absorbing chunks of Essex countryside like the stain of a spilt glass of red wine as it works its way across a white tablecloth – a patina of urban growth spilling from the Great Eastern Railway. The valley of the now-submerged Philley Brook was rapidly bricked over.

The streets are named variously after areas of West London or Southern Africa – Richmond and Twickenham are woven together with Rhodesia and Pretoria. I suppose this was a previous example of how new suburbs borrowed a slice of heritage from fashionable or resonant areas to inject kudos into the newly laid streets. Leytonstone might not have said much to the potential new residents of the late 19th century but Rhodesia and Pretoria spoke of colonies and the Boer War, Richmond and Twickenham the kind of respectable commuterville they couldn't afford but perhaps aspired to. Was that what was going on at East Village – not simply a village in the east but a facsimile of New York's uber-cool inner city hipster paradise of chai lattes, galleries, sexually ambiguous models dangling from fire escapes, dudes chatting beat poetry on the front step as the darling of the latest indie movie skips past with her rock star beau – but in Stratford rather than Manhattan?

Crossing Francis Road I passed from Leytonstone into Leyton. The Islamic Sharia Council sat on the corner of St George's Road opposite the Gurdwara – Islam, Sikhism and the patron saint of England snuggled up together in a quiet corner of East London. I wasn't here in search of religion though, but passing by the home of the great composer Cornelius Cardew who lived in Leyton Park Road and died not far away on Leyton High Road.

Cardew had been a student at the Royal College of Music who became one of the leading composers of the avant-garde music scene in the 1960s, a pioneer of 'graphic score' in place of the traditional musical notation. His compositions look more like circuit drawings of transistor radios than sheet music. The musician was thereby compelled to freely improvise and interpret the intent of the composer. His fame was such that Yoko Ono was a house guest at his Leyton home until she apparently became too annoying and overstayed her welcome. His Scratch Orchestra played at the Cultural Olympiad of the 1972 Munich Olympics, a move that ultimately tore the orchestra apart.

Cardew moved to Leyton in the early 1970s at the compulsion of the Maoist political sect he'd joined, the Communist Party of England (Marxist Leninist), who wanted him to forge links with the car workers at the Ford plant in Dagenham and help the fightback against the National Front who were increasingly active in the area. They sound like the kind of political group satirised in '70s comedies such as the Tooting Popular Front in Citizen Smith. Cardew rejected his avant-garde past and drew on traditional and folk music, and even formed a political rock group in his Leyton years. People's Liberation Music aimed to reach out to the masses on their own foot-tapping, head-bobbing terms.

In 2009 a group of local musicians honoured Cardew's connection to the area by performing his epic 9-hour The Great Learning in various locations around Leytonstone (only 12 minutes were played at the 1972 Proms at the Albert Hall) that at one point saw a musician playing a length of plastic ducting in St John's Church. I sat on the floor of the empty Woolworths on Leytonstone High Road while paragraphs of The Great Learning were sung in ethereal voices pacing down the ghosts of aisles where I'd variously purchased Power Rangers, a teapot, and a pear tree.

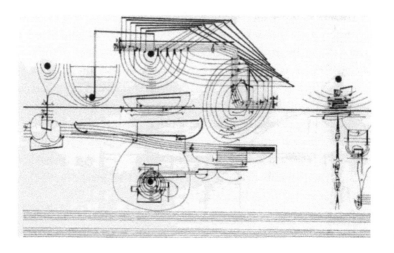

Jetfire orange lilies burst over a front garden wall in Leyton Park Road reaching for the sun that had beaten down relentlessly for the previous month. There's no plaque to mark the house where Cardew lived so I counted the flowers as a kind of karmic tribute to The Great Learning, which had been inspired by Confucianism.

Leyton High Road had grown into its Olympic face-lift. For a while the strip of shops from the tube station to Coronation Gardens wore their fancy new awnings like a ruffian forced into a smart suit for a wedding. One year on, the photographers led out here for the glossy mags in the pre-Olympic push had returned to Borough Market and it was clear the hand-painted signage and fresh awnings were here to stay and not just a loan for the duration of the Games.

Leyton Town Hall had also benefitted from a scrub down for the big event bringing out the russet glow of the red brick and the glimmer of the portland stone detailing. The building of the Town Hall was a grand statement of civic intent at a time when the new urban district spawned out of 'a place of gardens, parks and fields lying on the gentle slope between the Lea and the forest' as described by Weston in his history of the borough in 1921. The Saxon 'tun by the Lea' went through a rapid series of population bursts from the 1860s, growing from 5000 inhabitants to over 130,000 by 1920. The first Local Board was elected in 1873 and just over 20 years later they presided over the opening of this majestic Town Hall.

For 90 years the borough of Leyton occupied the centre of a municipal Venn diagram as part of the county of Essex and also the London postal districts. I get an odd thrill when finding traces of the old London boroughs that were mangled into new bodies by the Local Government Act of 1963, when Leyton was forced into a marriage with the boroughs of Chingford and Walthamstow to form the London borough of Waltham Forest. In 1965 the new Greater London was born – imperial London absorbing the urban and rural district councils into the federal entity of today.

Finding a borough of Leyton sign on a lamp-post declaring that dog 'fouling of a public footway' is punishable by a fine of forty shillings in order to preserve 'Good Rule and Government' produces a tingle down the spine, evidence of our benevolent 'creator'. The latest warning from Waltham Forest council declares that dog fouling is 'disgusting' and threatens to name and shame the perpetrators. Any idea of 'Good Rule and Government' was pushed aside when they started closing libraries and spending the money on firework displays and mugshots of pooches with transgressive toilet habits.

The list of lost boroughs reads like a roll call of vanished civilisations – Finsbury, Holborn, Shoreditch – Lyonesse, Eldorado, Atlantis. The stranded town halls, majestic municipal temples, stand as evidence of former glories, grand schemes and a belief in collective organisation for the greater good. The crests of the old orders survive etched into marble lobby floors, and engraved into oak notice boards where the founders of the boroughs have their names marked out in gold. Local historian David Boote records how one of the early chairmen of the council used the committee rooms of Leyton Town Hall for gatherings of the Guelph Masonic Lodge, a practice supposedly continued by subsequent Conservative councillors. The renaissance style architecture seems to lend itself to such a melding of the esoteric to the administrative.

A pub was occupying the front section of the Town Hall – the décor of the Leyton Technical had attempted to reflect the sensibility of its previous life. The entrance was adorned with a giant map of Greater London, the furniture a mismatched mash-up of rickety school desks, deep armchairs and committee tables; ale was served in pint mugs, pork pies were displayed under bell jars on the oak bar top. I've sat there late on a Monday or Tuesday night with a pint of Redemption Ale or an Adnams, a slice of Melton Mowbray on an antique plate and a packet of exotic flavoured crisps with the place to myself and it felt like the best private members club in the world. So I suppose there was an upside to the reorganisation of local government in London.

I found the spot on Leyton High Road where I think Cornelius Cardew was killed in a hit-and-run accident in the early hours of the morning on 13th December 1981 while walking back from Stratford station. Due to Cardew's political affiliations and the general paranoia that afflicts some people on the far left, it was rumoured that this was no accident due to poor visibility and icy roads as reported but was in fact an assassination by the East German secret service, the notorious Stasi. Other theories point the finger at MI5 or neo-Nazi groups. Cardew had recently attended political gatherings in Europe. He'd heckled Enoch Powell during a speech in the Houses of Parliament and been denounced as a traitor to the white race by the National Front. He'd been ruffling feathers all round. A zebra crossing is now scored upon the road to thwart any further black ops killings, black and white lines that appear like piano keys if you squint really hard and recall Cardew's Winter Potato No 1.

I walked in the trace of Cardew's last footsteps, along Leyton High Road towards Stratford and over the bridge where people had crowded to watch the Olympic fireworks. From here the M11 Link Road / A12 sweeps like a concrete park slide over the roof of the Velodrome to the towers on the horizon – the distant City edging ever closer.

On past Smart Look barbers, Cheap Calls, and Olympic Coffee with its shutters down. Loud reggae blared from a passing car. A lady in clip-clopping sandals ran for the No 158 bus to Chingford Mount where I'd walked to the other evening past the mothballed Walthamstow Dog Track.

The grassy bank on the side of Drapers Fields was sunburnt the colour of golden hay. In Temple Mills Lane I crossed the border into Newham. The border crossing brought forth an ominous dread of what lay ahead. There was something terrifying to me about the Olympic ghetto that I didn't yet understand: the scale, the immediacy and the ambition. Cardew's East German assassins would stop and admire the new citadel taking shape across the road. It felt like looking down the gullet of a dystopian future, a place where we'll be penned in and forced to shop and watch the X-Factor. The fear washed over me till I noticed that the previously vacant Wheeler's Bar was being squatted – perhaps there was hope in this small rebellion against the developers.

A road to nowhere with no name led to a hump in the road offering a panoramic view of old and new Stratford – Westfield to the left, to the right the spire of West Ham Church, the roof of the Town Hall and the sixties and seventies tower blocks screened by a shoal of commissioned metallic fish to divert attention away from the past. It made me think of Slough – or in the bright sunshine the Beverley Centre in LA. People bobbed along the footbridge inside an iron and glass promenade, insect-like in their proportions relative to the buildings around them. This new world was not built to human scale but in the proportions of biblical Nephilim, otherworldly giants with a taste for designer clothes. In the murky reaches of the internet you find legions of grown adults who fervently believe not only that these 9-foot tall coneheads walked the earth but that they are soon to return. Westfield is here to welcome them back – a temple for the Nephilim – but as crazy as that is, it makes far more sense than what it appears to be. Shops don't need to be that big.

Planes sliced across the skyline on the approach run to City Airport. What was this London I saw before me with the concrete dildos poking out of marsh mud intersected with rising highways. This wasn't the London of Mick Jagger in Performance or The Beatles crossing Abbey Road, it wasn't any recognisable London of the past. It was more like a poor facsimile of the back end of Houston, Texas circa 1985.

I met Chris outside the Theatre Royal, Stratford East and we wandered up Angel Lane towards the site of Clays Lane. Chris was one of 450 people who lived around ten courtyards – all single people, two-thirds nominated by local authorities, the other third students. Each of the courtyards elected representatives to the management committee who took care of the day-to-day running of the estate. Chris told me how Clays Lane had been under attack for a while – first an attempted aggressive takeover by the Peabody Trust, then a compulsory purchase order for the building of Stratford City, what we now know simply as Westfield.

We passed the Travellers' site near Temple Mills Lane. The Travellers had also been on the plot and were moved as a community to the other side of the road. The Clays Lane residents weren't so lucky. They had wanted to relocate as a group but as Chris said, 'Have you ever tried to get 450 people to agree on anything?'. He spent weeks and months locked in meetings with the London Development Agency (LDA) but with the Labour Party at the time so enthusiastic about the Olympics, local councillors and MPs were far from sympathetic to their cause. 'Who cares about a bunch of hippies and some students, that's the way they saw it. That's the way it was I suppose but what's wrong with being a hippy or a student', he lamented. There was the possibility of a site down at Albert Docks, at that time deserted and unwanted, but the consensus was that it was too far away from Stratford and under the flight path of City airport.

We looked across Drapers Fields that had been annexed during the Olympics but now returned to the community as a sports field. Chris pointed out where the estate was located on the far side of the fields and railway lines in a turning off Temple Mills Lane. He found it difficult to pinpoint from this distance and with Temple Mills Lane still blocked off, but it was basically in the footprint of the celebrated Velodrome, the scene of so much Olympic triumph and chest-beating. When you looked at the site the way it was before the Olympics with the railway yards and the cold storage depot that left permafrost stretching eight feet beneath ground, I said to Chris that it was difficult to over-romanticise it. Chris agreed but added, 'The biggest tragedy was the breakup of a community of over 400 people'.

Chris had done so many walks and interviews about the area since he was evicted that he didn't know what to make of it now except that he missed it, and missed the Eastway cycle track that was nearby. He'd started off in London over West in Ladbroke Grove in 1971 when it was cheap, then moved to Chepstow Villas in Notting Hill, all divided up into little rooms full of people from everywhere looking for somewhere cheap to live. An area of London that has since changed beyond all recognition from that transient radical '70s heyday.

Chris had never even been to Stratford before he moved into Clays Lane. 'I believed that the earth was flat beyond the Bow Flyover, there be dragons, primordial marshlands', he growled in his rich voice. Chris wasn't the only one: when the Olympics was announced the LDA didn't even know where Clays Lane was. He said he had to meet them at the station and take them there.

To do a full circuit of the Olympic site involved going all the way up Leyton High Road to Ruckholt Road, named after one of the old manors of Leyton. This was a walk Chris had done more times than he cared to remember, 'thousands of times', but most notably with artist Lucy Harrison as part of the Mapping Your Manor project. Each time he repeated the walk he noticed small changes, changes that will continue for some years yet and you can well believe that Chris will keep touring the site for as long as he's able, keeping a careful eye on the powers who booted him out of his home.

Opposite New Spitalfields Market we tried to locate the point where Temple Mills Lane joined the Eastway. I recognised where Eton Manor Cricket Club once stood from my first walk round this way when I moved to Leytonstone, hunting down locations from Paul Kelly's film What Have You Done Today Mervyn Day? in the winter of 2006.

When I moved east to Leytonstone I bonded with my new home by organising a screening in my local pub of Mervyn Day alongside Leytonstone film-maker John Smith's The Black Tower and Blight, and fellow Leytonstonian Ian Bourn's Black, White & Green – The Way of Pie – shot in the pie and mash shop at Harrow Green, Leytonstone. A collaboration with pop maestros Saint Etienne, Paul Kelly's film is set in the lower Lea Valley on the day after the announcement in summer 2005 that London would host the 2012 Olympics. Shot mostly around Stratford and Bow, Kelly described What Have You Done Today Mervyn Day? as being like an obituary to the birthplace of the 20th century.

The film uses the fictional device of a paper boy doing his rounds who allows his sense of curiosity to lead him on a journey through the ruination of an area that gave the world plastic and petrol. A radio news bulletin establishes the time and place, 7th July 2005, a day of national celebration and disaster. 'The Lea

Valley. A river runs through it. You can catch a kingfisher if you're lucky. Catch it while you can, it's all gonna go', narrates Canning Town's David Essex.

Paul Kelly's camerawork framed this blighted landscape in all its rusting glory, the wide skies calling to mind the more epic landscapes of Russia and Outback Australia. Aerial shots of the Stratford skyline predicting the mini-City that is to come. A Geoffrey Fletcher-esque recording of small features such as letter-boxes, drainpipes, and graffiti (Fletcher was fond of gas lighting and the fittings in public lavatories). Quick flashes of street signage – Pudding Mill Lane, Marshgate Lane Industrial Area. Derelict red-brick factories manage to look like the ruins of ancient Rome as Mervyn cycles past on his rounds, paperboys themselves being an anachronism. As Mervyn gazes across the Thames at the Millennium Dome the warning was clear enough, but as the narration reminds us 'The Lea Valley has always been about change'.

The removal of geographical reference points had Chris stumped – for a man who knew every kerbside weed and discarded lorry tyre, the landscape has been wiped clean, the mental maps erased, a blank slate for the developers to write their own histories. The Eastway Cycle Track was shunted out further east to Hainault, another community displaced. We got buzzed on the footpath by a cyclist who seemed unfamiliar with the braking mechanism on her oversized mock postman's bike. 'Sorry', she called out in a posh voice as she hurtled past. 'There's the cycle path', he retorted. 'What is it with middle class people' he said to me.

We cut through the woods at Hackney Wick over a carpet of fluffy white poplar seeds, it was like walking through the thick snow of fairytales. Shards of sunlight sliced through the leaves. We cast a glance at the old Matchbox Cars factory: do I even have to mention that it'd been converted into flats?

These circuits would soon be ending when routes across the park opened up, and aside from Chris you wondered how many people would continue to circle the park examining it from the periphery, maintaining the link between the hoopla inside and the realities of the world beyond. From the time the blue fence was first erected it became a form of ritual to circumnavigate the Olympic zone. Numerous processions were recorded. Hackney's shaman Iain Sinclair wrote about his walk with photographer Stephen Gill, and returned in the summer of 2012 with film-maker Andrew Kötting in a swan-shaped pedalo that had sailed an epic journey along inland waterways from Hastings only to be thwarted in the Lea by the security barriers across the water. There was ex-Pogues musician Jem Finer's legion of trumpeters trying to bring the fence down as the Walls of Jericho had been toppled. Today we have neither instruments nor novelty watercraft, just the plodding of our footsteps. The days of creative opposition were over.

Over the Hackney Cut was one of the most successful Olympic protests in the form of the custom-built premises of H Forman & Son, previously located in the middle of the Olympic site. Forman refused to move. According to Chris, he argued that his fish had to be on the table at the Savoy at eight in the morning so the proposed relocation to Essex was out of the question. Furthermore, his family had been in the area for generations producing the finest smoked fish in London. What we were looking at was the result of his resistance – a huge new space, built to his own specifications with a restaurant and gallery on site. 'Forman was a hero to us at Clays Lane', said Chris. Mr Forman was one of the Olympic winners who didn't need to stand on a podium or have his face on a cereal packet.

A fisherman called us across to look at the size of the carp sliding around near the lock. There had been great shoals of them when I'd passed this way on the previous walk. We remarked at how clean the water looked. Just two weeks later the long dry spell was ended by a torrential downpour that washed a toxic cocktail of pollutants off the roads and out of the soil into the Lea killing thousands of fish that floated on the surface as if struck by an Old Testament curse. For all the attempts to greenwash the developments around Stratford it only took a thunderstorm to bring home the reality of the effect on the river and its tributaries. The Pudding Mill Stream that ran through the park had already been consigned to the long list of London's lost rivers.

We climbed up onto the Greenway. As well as being the final leg of the circuit on this Olympic traipse it formed the spine of one of Chris's guided walks that went around Beckton and the Woolwich Ferry. I told him about my trek from the ferry through Bostall Woods to the Dartford Salt Marshes the previous summer and wondered if he tired of continuously treading the same route. 'You have to keep walking the same walks over and over again, like a mantra', he said. It was a beautiful idea to ponder as we passed the piles of dirt still being shifted around, the walk as a spiritual device. Instead of a shaven-headed monk high in the Tibetan mountains cross-legged in a temple, two long-haired blokes schlepping around a building site in East London – every bit as transcendental if not more so. The path to enlightenment starts just outside your front door.

The raised aspect of this Victorian sewage pipe turned heritage walkway gave us a view across the rooftops of what remained of old industrial Stratford. Chris pointed out that this had always been a productive and profitable area. He would walk up Marshgate Lane counting the small businesses – there was all sorts of stuff and hundreds round Carpenters Road, he said. What has replaced it? – minimum wage jobs at Westfield. I wondered about the future of what was being created in Stratford. 'No one cares about that, dude – it's all about now. Even Clays Lane had a million pound turn-over – it might have been a co-op full of hippies but it was still a business.'

We descended from the Greenway and worked our way round into Carpenters Estate. 'I've never been down here', I said. 'Nor have most people mate', Chris replied. This was always a bit of forgotten backwater – even for someone living nearby on Clays Lane. Carpenters successfully fought off an attempt by University College, London to build a campus on the site, which would have amounted to another tight-knit community being broken up and displaced, shunted away from the prime development zone. Long settled working-class communities didn't fit into Theresa May, Boris Johnson and the LDA's plan for the Olympic legacy. When Johnson was asked whether 30% was a suitable amount of social housing for the Olympic Park developments he said that it sounded about right because 'It should be somewhere people want to move "to not from"'. A local community worker handing out fliers for a fundraiser overheard our conversation and came over for a chat. Although people had started to drift away from the two tower blocks that were hidden behind enormous advertising hoardings during the Games they were now being moved back in during that summer of 2013. UCL had retreated, stung by the backlash against their plans, taken aback by accusations of social cleansing and elitism. You sensed that this may have been a tactical withdrawal but the community worker assured us Carpenters was here to stay. Most of the people here had never lived anywhere else. Hidden from the outside world in a compact series of cul-de-sacs it had a left-behind feel of a time not so long ago when this was the way that the majority of people in Britain lived. When I was growing up on an estate in the 1970s over 70% of the population lived in council housing. The planners and politicians who would rather have a university campus of transient fee-paying students seemed to struggle to see the value of communities like Carpenters and Clays Lane.

We departed the estate trying to locate the source of an incredible aroma of roasting coffee beans, an example of the type of small businesses that thrived in this landscape. As we followed the path round behind Stratford station, Chris told me about an old industrial estate between Canning Town and the back of Bow that was still going strong, great working men's cafés. 'We'll do it one day mate', he said as we parted. I said we'd better hurry, plans were being laid for every patch of land in the lower Lea Valley. There was a land grab going on, a real estate gold rush. Ten years on we still haven't done that walk together.

I continued to stalk East Village through the dark winter months looking for lights coming in on the windows to signal habitation. I'd registered as a prospective tenant and the more the pleasant young salespeople rang me to get me to sign up for a flat, the more I became seduced by the idea of being one of the first residents in London's newest neighbourhood. I eventually told one woman on the third call about my tweet that had started the process and that

I'd only registered for a flat for research purposes. Even more reason to take a flat she persisted.

By February 2014 the lights were still out in the East Village. I'd get excited by the occasional illumination before realising it was a lone light in an unpeopled stairwell being triggered by the passing ghosts of failed Olympians. The more I passed down the few streets that were open leading to Westfield the more the idea grew that perhaps, just perhaps this wouldn't be a Mega City ghetto without Judge Dredd for protection but could be an interesting place to live despite having all the ambience of the set of a zombie movie. I made it my habit to catch the new 339 bus from the stop in Liberty Bridge Road at the heart of the development figuring that cold wet Tuesday evenings were when places really came alive. I saw the first lights come on, heard music from the inaugural housewarming parties, saw people lugging bags of possessions into the lifts. It was slowly becoming a place.

Confident that routes into the park would be open from Ruckholt Road, restoring the old passage of Temple Mills Lane, one Sunday afternoon in 2014 I promised the family a shortcut to the log cabin café. The road led to a security-protected dead end. We pushed on past the piles of earth that became the Chobham Manor 'village', and I wondered if this vista would ever change, the Olympics seemed like a dream.

The signage screamed at pedestrians not to walk – at one point we became marooned on a traffic island – two adults, two boys and a pug terrified to move with cement mixers hurtling past to hell. Following the signage to the letter would have meant finding a tree to climb then radio in for an airlift out of this autogeddon. It looked as though Chris's circuit was still the only viable route into the park before we ignored a Keep Out sign and ventured down Waterden Road. A jogger puffed past. Then someone with a pram. Life in the park. The boys rolled down the steep banks, Rocky gambolled in the grass and we spat out clods of pollution beside the calming waters of the Lea.

Then the route East-West slowly opened, at first along a caged walkway that skirted the Olympic Stadium and came out on White Post Lane in Hackney Wick linking up with the historic White Lion running track where the Native American athlete Deerfoot raced in 1862.

In early spring I became one of the first civilians to walk along Honour Lea Avenue, finally open to the public eight months after I'd toured the Village. It was a peculiar sensation. I began to understand the horror I felt at times to perhaps be similar to what people must've experienced when they saw the first streets laid out in the fields of Perivale and Sudbury Hill. Here we were bearing witness to the next great expansion of London.

CHAPTER 3

THE NEW ERA / A NEW HOPE

As much as I wanted to escape the shadow cast eastwards by Stratford City, I was trapped inside its gravitational vortex. I felt like Han Solo, Chewbacca, Luke, Princess Leia, and Obi-Wan Kenobi aboard the Millennium Falcon being sucked inside the bowels of the Death Star in Star Wars: A New Hope. Perhaps it was best to adopt the Jedi approach and submit to the tractor beam and destroy the enemy from within. So I allowed myself to spend hours at Westfield browsing camera gear at Currys, flicking through the shelves at GAME with the kids, and working through the polyglot selection of cuisines in the Food Court. Meanwhile, I routinely stalked the streets of East Village day and night sampling the ambiences of the 339 bus stop on a wet Tuesday evening, and the view from the Teletubbies mound on windy Sunday afternoons. I made short video diaries charting the subtle changes taking place.

One morning I joined the Greenway at Hackney Wick – the brass letters embossed into the granite almost matching the opening title font of Star Wars. From the elevated walkway, the westwards view towards Bow looked across a newly laid plain of concrete, presumably the foundations of the Pudding Mill development. The mounds of earth that were here when I logged the location at the end of 2013 had been cleared but little other major work appeared to have been done during the intervening months. The Pudding Mill Stream has been lost somewhere beneath ground, filled in, erased from the map. A blank canvas cleared for the developers to imprint their 'vision', peeling back the layers of history so that the only map I could find that made any sense was from the late 18th century showing the River Lea meandering across Bow Marsh and through Old Ford to the strip of buildings and mills along the Stratford turnpike road. I watched builders constructing a wooden replica of Newton's cottage at Carpenters Lock – the past brought back to life as temporary public sculpture.

The intensity of this engagement went up a notch in the autumn of 2014 when a group of young mothers from Stratford squatted an empty property on the Carpenters Estate and opened a social space. A tweet from an old City Poly comrade circa 1990, Kevin 'Copwatcher' Blowe, alerted me to the Focus E15 occupation. It seemed that the optimism of the community worker I'd met the previous summer, talking of people moving back to the estate, had been short-lived and now Focus E15 were campaigning to 'Repopulate the Carpenters Estate' and made a call-out for assistance. Thinking that a trainee Urban Druid would be of little use I offered my services as a film-maker, not the introspective pocket camera diaries shot at the 339 bus stop, but something to help amplify the cause. Also, Russell Brand had recently taken an interest in trying to help the residents of the New Era Estate in Hoxton who were facing enormous rent hikes and inevitable eviction. Russell had asked if I could get on board, so I suggested he come along to the E15 Open House on Carpenters with some of the New Era residents. This forgotten backwater in Stratford was about to become the epicentre of global media attention.

It was easy to find the two-storey semi being occupied in the middle of the estate. Two large green fabric banners puffed out the width of the building in the breeze spelt out the straight-forward message – 'THESE PEOPLE NEED HOMES – THESE HOMES NEED PEOPLE'. From the open windows hung more banners in colourful nursery school fonts – 'SOCIAL HOUSING NOT SOCIAL CLEANSING', 'Focus E15 Mums – Keep Us in London', and 'SHERIFF OF NEWHAM – ROBIN THE POOR' – a reference to the Mayor of Newham Sir Robin Wales, who'd been captured on camera verbally attacking the Focus E15 Mums when they approached him at a Family Day. Kicking around on the lawn looking up towards the windows was the Guardian journalist Zoe Williams: nobody else appeared to be around. The Guardian had run a story about the occupation and the paper were seemingly adopting the cause, belatedly waking up to the housing crisis in London now that it was lapping up against the front porches of the middle classes. It was the beginning of a sur-real morning – standing on the lawn of a squatted council house on the Carpenters Estate with the favourite columnist of the North London Chianti set. Eventually, we attracted the attention of some people inside and we were led through a metal squatters' door at the rear of the house.

The occupiers were clearly at pains to show the house in its do-mestic guise rather than as purely a centre of resistance. Kids' toys were neatly stacked in a corner, fresh flowers in a vase on the win-dow sill, hot drinks were offered. A framed sign on the wall spelt out the credo, 'United we are strong. Secure housing for all. London for everyone not just the rich. We don't want our neighbourhoods to be gentrified and entire communities evicted. We want quality affordable housing for all.'

Then a paragraph pinned to the wall explaining that Focus E15 was the name of the Mother and Baby Unit from which the women had been evicted and offered alternative accommodation in Manchester, Hastings or Birmingham. Meanwhile perfectly good homes on the Carpenters Estate were being left to stand empty until Newham council could find a suitable buyer for the land. Tenanted social housing didn't appear to be in the plan for the new Stratford, didn't align with the vision of international university campuses and prestigious cultural institutions. It's too much of a reminder of Stratford's industrial working past. I decided to warn Zoe Williams of Russell's impending arrival and the chaos that was likely to ensue.

Russell arrived swagged up on the Carpenters in a black Merc driven by his loyal chauffeur Mick, who'd been driving Russell since the My Booky Wook tour and had driven him ever since. Draped in designer black and hidden by shades Russell was accompanied by a relatively modest entourage compared to the peak Hollywood years – the inevitable cameraman, ever-present hair and make-up lady doubling as PA, and Danielle from the New Era Estate. They unloaded bulging bags of shopping from the boot of Mick's car and lugged it up the stairs. The tone of excitement rose in the house from grim determination to squeaky fandom as everybody clustered around Russell who was in the kitchen handing out Jaffa Cakes. A journalist from the Independent pretended to continue her interview with one of the activists who was helping run the Open House but her eyes were following Russell from the kitchen to the hallway. This was a celebrity appearance as activism – instead of opening a Lidl, Russell was endorsing an occupation.

Soon everyone gathered in the one room – Zoe Williams seemed to have accepted her role now as witness to the spectacle. The general tone of the Mums' voices rose several octaves, they were no longer scowling but beaming smiles and giggling. Gareth the cameraman shot everything for an episode of Russell's YouTube series The Trews (True News – names had never been his strong point). The resistance had just become a peculiar kind of council estate press junket.

By the time Jasmine from the E15 Mums took Russell outside for a walkabout on the estate word had spread and it became a full-on autograph and selfie session with Russell trying to use the opportunity to elicit information about the estate and the residents' plight. We were told how tenants didn't want to leave Carpenters. Some of those hanging back around the periphery of the scrum expressed reservations about the presence of the Focus E15 Mums, the loud parties, comedy nights, steady stream of scruffy looking protesters making their way to the occupation. They were merely trying to get on with their lives – their resistance expressed simply by staying in their homes. The protest of the Open House would inevitably end, the media return to Guardian Towers and Shoreditch lofts but the surviving residents of the Carpenters Estate would remain.

Newham council took legal action against the occupation and a court date was set. We returned to take part in a protest outside Newham magistrates court on Romford Road. This time when I arrived at the house not only was Russell there but so were several camera crews, including a documentary team that had flown in from South Africa. This squatted semi-detached on the Carpenters Estate had made the London housing crisis international news. Journos and floating activists milled around the estate wondering where the hell they were and whether this was the true Olympic legacy. The burghers of Newham and City Hall had always intended that London 2012 would project Stratford onto the international stage but not as the base camp for an assault on just the kind of speculative development they were hoping to encourage.

The scene at the courthouse was buoyant. Around two hundred people thronged on the pavement. Colourful banners were held aloft by a cohort consisting of small left-wing and anarchist groups, lone freelancers, and locals who'd picked up the story. In the crowd I spotted trade unionists I knew, old comrades from City Poly Labour Club circa 1990 still fighting the good fight, supporters of local non-league club Clapton FC. Russell was thrown straight into a media throng more intense than the red carpet at the Oscars. BBC London moved in first, a Sky News lens loomed across to steal the shot, ITV News hovered in the background. Then there were of course the cluster of YouTube video activists with varying levels of kit from selfie-stick smart-phone wands, through holiday camcorders upgraded with oversized microphones, to the serious DSLR shooters sitting aloft body-mounted rigs. For today the alternative media held parity with the legacy broadcasters. Guardian mouthpiece Owen Jones turned up on a bike and was immediately surrounded by angry student journos who seemed to see Jones as representing the enemy, although his actual crime had never been clear to me other than popping up on the TV too often saying the things that they parroted in empty meeting rooms. Jolyon Rubinstein from BBC Comedy show The Revolution Will Not Be Televised was eagerly buzzing around with a crew – he too was following the new zeitgeist movement for a TV doc. Amongst it all the Focus E15 Mums looked slightly dazed and lost, they'd been the people nobody wanted to think about, and now they were the new media sensation, the One Direction of street activism.

I joined the Focus E15 group inside the courthouse – which compared to the chaos outside was a place of calm. Even looking at people chewing on their nails awaiting their hearing was relaxing. A lawyer had stepped forward pro bono in the intervening days, you could sense the momentum of the growing tide. Outside I bumped into a neighbour of mine, a middle-aged cycling Pixie woman, a kind of urban Puck manifesting out of the brickwork to deliver cryptic statements about the movements of the stars and the phases of the moon. She'd been supporting the Focus E15 cause from the beginning since encountering them at their regular Stratford street stall. She told me that at a previous court appearance just a few weeks before, the supporters outside the court had numbered in single figures – now Sky News alone had a larger crew than the first protest could muster. And this in the space of a few weeks – where would the movement be in a year's time people wondered?

I headed back into the throng and moved among the familiar faces of campaigns past dating back over 25 years. I used to walk past this building every day when I first moved to London aged 18 and shacked up living the scumbag polytechnic dream inspired by The Young Ones in a terraced house just off Romford Road. I reflected that I hadn't come far – and was glad of it.

Then Russell emerged on the court steps with Jasmine Stone of the E15 Mums and she read her statement to the assembled throng. They'd agreed by consent to end their occupation but not to drop their demands that the Carpenters Estate be repopulated with residents given secure social tenancies. She signed off by declaring 'This is the beginning of the end of the housing crisis'.

The next battleground had already been declared. Russell was keen to help the residents of the New Era Estate somehow and wanted me to join the cause. Carpenters was on my beat, Hoxton was not an area that I would normally delve into, it felt as if its myths past and present had been flogged to death from Gangster Lore through Brit Art to Digital Hipsterville. But that was a sign of my ignorance.

After a chaotic meeting in the back room of the Stags Head pub with a group of the residents plus an A-Team of people Russell had only met via email, I was appointed head of the campaign. I'd never been asked – people's homes were at stake. I hastily and properly passed the baton back to the residents – they'd run their own campaign – we'd help in any way we could, in my case with a camera.

It was a familiar scene – backrooms of Hackney pubs, political discussions, planning campaigns, attempting to save treasured community assets. This had been my constituency in the early '90s when I ran a Hackney Labour Party ward from my squatted council flat. I went to a meeting just like this one about every other night. Even Russell's presence wasn't incongruous – we met when I was writing and directing political satire on the London Fringe. We moved from the Riverside Studios to the backrooms and upstairs of pubs – one of our early ventures was in the Hackney Empire Studio. I couldn't help noticing the stage at one end of the room directly in Russell's eyeline and wondering if this would be a good place for a gig.

The New Era crusade was a revival of old times with Russell – bypassing the TV shows, supermodel snogs, Hollywood, to his quest to save Spitalfields Market from redevelopment in 2002 – a documentary project that ended with Russell entering rehab under duress with the edit incomplete.

He'd managed to blag an envelope of cash from his agent to make a TV pilot with a whiff of interest from a hot production company. His idea was to take on the Spitalfields Development Corporation who were planning on converting the old fruit and veg market into a shopping mall and office complex. For a crazy week, along with a band of collaborators he'd assembled, we troubled various members of the development consortium and Tower Hamlets council, on occasion with Russell dressed as the Elephant Man or Jack the Ripper. Most memorably, he interviewed the head of the development corporation with a glove puppet of the Devil. It was an introduction into the murky world where property development interfaces with local government. 'Off the record' rooftop briefings filled us in on backroom deals, planning gain and Section 106 funding was explained, the power struggle emerging between the City of London and Canary Wharf provided the backdrop. We were given helpful advice by members of the City of London Police who showed us the brass strip in the pavement on Bishopsgate where their jurisdiction ended. The innocuous band of metal on the ground that thousands of people walked across every day marked the frontline of a border war being fought between two of the wealthiest institutions on the planet. And we thought we could take them on with a video camera, some bad costumes, and a cluster of pithy quips.

The manifesto I wrote with Russell, appended to the back of the TV pitch document declared:

1. We believe in the use of Comedy Terrorism
2. We are the Harlequins of the revolution
3. The current Parliament of Idiots must be overthrown and replaced with an elected Central Committee of Clowns
4. The new political order will be made up of Minstrels instead of Ministers
5. We are inspired by: the Minstrels of Berne, the Mummers of England, Italian jongleurs of the Middle Ages, Lenny Bruce, Dario Fo, The Simpsons, South Park, Jackass, the Biotic Baking Brigade, Ralph Steadman, Steve Bell, and the experience of the Soapbox Cabaret.

I have no idea what Channel 4 made of this madness but a year later Russell was announced as the host of Big Brother's Big Mouth.

A lot had happened since then. Gigs in pubs had moved into arenas, the streets of East London slow faded to Los Angeles. Movies, tours, national scandals, marriage, divorce, kids, and network TV shows. Clean and sober, discharged from the Hollywood asylum, New Era could be that, for the estate, for Russell, perhaps even for London.

If activism in 2014 was about anything getting your message out was key and social media provided the platforms. My hacked-together video journals, quickly assembled and disseminated, could have some use – particularly when magnified by the lens of Russell's colossal social media presence. Russell had embarked on an interesting new career trajectory as a YouTuber, daily tearing apart the multiple conceits of the newspapers and Fox News – something he'd witnessed first-hand as red-top fodder in his womanising celebrity years. It'd proved a rich source of material for stand-up shows down the years and now back in Blighty with an audience eager to hear his opinions spitting out down the internet every day unfiltered, social media proved the perfect forum. The shift from Hollywood to Google had just been a case of following the flow of power – from movies to the internet and direct communication with your audience.

Returning to the estate the following week to shoot the first videos I felt twinges of familiarity, odd buildings linked to memories that for all the turfing out of the drawers, boxes, and supermarket carrier bags littering my psyche I couldn't quite retrieve. It must have been from my time in Hackney South and Shoreditch Labour Party, the constituency covering New Era, the door knocking on wet November days like these. This was the in-between stretch of Kingsland Road – 'outta' Shoreditch and not yet Dalston. An area developers were desperate to rebrand 'Hoxditch'.

This is an ancient district, sat on the Roman Ermine Street. It's mentioned in the Domesday Book and the land here was owned by

the Bishops of London until at least the 14th century. Writing in
the 12th century William Fitzstephen described 'the fields for pasture, and open meadows, very pleasant, into which the river waters
do flow, and mills are turned about with a delightful noise. Next
lieth a great forest, in which are woody places and for game...'

Hoxton was noted for its medicinal wells and was developed as
a retreat for city merchants in the Tudor era and became known
as a place of leisure and market gardens around the time of the
Restoration. The Regent's Canal created another significant thoroughfare bisecting the area bringing warehouses and industrial
units along the towpath. The population of Shoreditch boomed,
the market gardens were trampled and by 1861 it had a population
of 129,364. George Gissing, used Hoxton in his 'Story of English
Socialism', Demos, published in 1886, describing the canal 'stag-
nating in utter foulness between coal-wharfs and builders' yards'.
Shoreditch and Hoxton had become a slum.

Estates such as New Era were part of a 20th century renaissance instigated by Shoreditch Borough Council, the slums were
cleared with the aid of the Luftwaffe during the Second World War
and replaced with blocks of modern flats. But now another blitz
approached.

The three women at the centre of the resistance had assembled
to make the first video. Lyndsay, Lindsey, and Danielle hunched
together on a sofa so I could get them all in frame. They spelt out
the basic lie of the land for the YouTube audience. How the estate had been put up for sale by the charitable trust that owned it
and then bought by a consortium of private investors that included
Britain's richest MP, the Tory Richard Benyon, and US based property developers Westbrook. Rents had instantly been raised from
standard social rates by £200 per month and were set to rise again
the following year to market value, which in Hoxton was around

£600 per week for a 2-bedroom flat at that time. The assumption made by the new owners was that unable to afford the new rents, the residents would simply leave. It was a fundamental misreading of the strength of character and community on the New Era. What followed was a campaign the like they could never have imagined when doing yet another property deal, one that put them on the front pages and in the broadcast news and over the course of the next eight weeks drew attention from around the world.

Next day I was back at New Era talking to Patricia in her kitchen. All the flats I'd visited were immaculately kept and well-maintained. I was later told that tenants took great pride in keeping their homes in good condition paying for repairs and renovations themselves, installing new kitchens and bathrooms out of their own pockets while the landlord had allowed the car park to become full of potholes.

Patricia had lived on the New Era for 14 years, moving in to care for her elderly mother-in-law when she became ill, her husband having grown up on the estate. She told me how the previous owners, the Levy family, were 'socially-minded people' who'd kept the rents low, and that family members often stood a good chance of being allocated flats in order to keep families together. There were three generations of some families on the estate. When Richard Benyon turned up on the New Era Patricia had told him, 'I thought I'd be leaving here in a box, not a removal van'. Residents were informed straight away they'd have to pay market rents. She recounted how she saw the young people of Hoxton and Shoreditch in a constant state of transit pulling trolley bags through the streets from one flat to the next: 'All everybody talks about round here is their rent and how they can't pay it. The council have a moral duty to people who have been born and bred to help us stay in our homes, we're a community round here,' she declared leant against

52

the sink. Patricia's son lives in the estate. The council asked him if he'd live with his mother. 'He's 47' she says in an incredulous voice, 'and then they said to him "Would your mum like to move to Clacton?" It's like somebody's thrown a black net over the flats.'

The Hoxton spirit is strong, there'll be a fight, one that will draw in thousands Patricia told the camera, 'It's not just us – we're going to join up. Who's going to be living in London? Only the very rich.'

Sitting in her lounge we were joined by Danielle with her young son, and Mary with her 44-year old son Bill, a single dad of two boys. Mary had been born in Whiston Road just the other side of Kingsland Road, never leaving these tight few streets in Hoxton. She couldn't believe they were being forced out for people who'd be using it as a convenient stop-over, not families, not people making homes and a community, but simply the restless rich. She hoped the Benyons would see what they were doing to people's lives and change their minds. She'd been to a sympathetic Hackney council's Housing Office, at pains to point out how helpful they'd been, but all they could potentially offer was sheltered accommodation. She found it frustrating to see her childhood turf of Whiston Road being redeveloped, homes were available, but only for the highest bidder. Mary's son, Bill picked his kids up from the local school every day. His rent would be raised to £650 per week, rates that nobody on the estate could afford. 'I'd live in a tent on Shoreditch Green if I had to just to be near my kids, don't know what to do next, we're going to fight all the way.'

Finally I dropped by Ozan whose hairdresser's salon occupied one of the retail units built into the exterior of the New Era on Whitmore Road. The shop-keepers had been given notice, told to find alternative locations. After 15 years, for Ozan leaving Hoxton would mean starting again. The customers didn't want him to go far. 'We're like a big family with the clients', people who came there as kids now bring their children to have their hair cut. 'People have changed since I came. I'm a humanist, I like everyone.'

Making my way back down Orsman Road there was an overpowering sense that the heart was being ripped out of this tight-knit community that possessed all the values we are told to cherish and promote. But it was also clear that nobody was going to be leaving the New Era without one hell of a fight.

The video I produced had the desired effect of raising the profile of the campaign with the added push of Russell's vast social media following. The online petition grew and grew with people flocking to the cause from across the globe. A protest was called that for some reason that I can't recall (and didn't catch on) Russell decided should have a Dickensian theme. It could have been an association with our Spitalfields Market campaign. When it came to the day, among the protestors gathered outside Ozan's hairdresser's on Whitmore Road Russell stood out in his Bill Sykes / Artful Dodger garb.

The throng that stopped the traffic as it moved through Hoxton into De Beauvoir Town was a coalition of New Era residents, the usual left-wing groups, trade unionists, teachers, Russell Brand fans, and representatives from residents' groups from across London. I met people that day whose campaigns I'd later be drawn to aid with the only real tools I had of use – my camera and a YouTube channel.

The aim was to march on the De Beauvoir home of Richard Benyon, frontman for the Westbrook operation. From a campaigning point-of-view he was a gift, the wicked wealthy Tory MP with his enormous country pile heartlessly evicting working-class families in the weeks before Christmas. Like Russell's costume it was oddly Dickensian.

An eviction notice was pinned to the doors of his offices. Lyndsay made a rousing speech from the steps to the assembled throng: natural leaders were emerging. The press had picked up on the story, photographers and camera crews crowded in. By the end of the campaign Lyndsay standing and addressing a crowd with arm upraised would become an iconic image with tinges of Boudicca.

Then it was on to Benyon's townhouse – the kind of grand Hackney home built for 19th century gentry as a country retreat that was now changing hands for millions. Scaffolding conveniently erected around the front of the house was too much for Russell to resist and with the aid of a childhood friend, now a firefighter, he scaled it to serve the eviction notice and then wave a banner to give the press their image for the next day's papers.

The Benyons bailed from the New Era deal pretty swiftly after that. As hoped, they didn't need the bother of comedians clambering up the outside of their London pad. But that meant all was in the hands of the American property molochs, Westbrook. Could they be reasoned with?

The community banded tightly together. Media interest grew. The activist community rallied. Housing was the hot topic being debated on radio phone-ins and newspaper columns every day. On a trip to New York Russell was able to enlist the support of New York Mayor Bill De Blasio who'd dealt with Westbrook in the Big Apple. Mayor of London Boris Johnson, was consequently shamed to respond, reluctantly shifted his fringe and urged that a deal be struck. The petition grew and grew until it was time to be delivered to No.10 Downing Street. There'd be a march from Westbrook's London HQ in Berkeley Square to Whitehall. There was a sense that this was it.

There was a nervous muted mood in the estate carpark as we mustered before boarding the coach, like you imagine there was in the camp the morning before a battle in the Middle Ages. Instead of swords and spears, placards and banners were handed out and inspected. Chants were rehearsed instead of war cries. The film director Michael Winterbottom was mooching about with a crew – capturing scenes for a feature documentary he was making with Russell, timed to come out before the 2015 General Election. I saw Patricia and Lyndsay – they were optimistic, focused, ready for what was to come.

The kids were having the day off school giving the coach ride through the City of London the vibe of a school trip – Hula Hoops were munched – I even brought a packed lunch. Winterbottom's cameraman attempted to get some shots with his enormous shoulder-mounted camera, people sang and waved out the window to well-wishers on the pavement. Word started to arrive that there was a huge noisy crowd already assembled in Berkeley Square. Mayfair hadn't witnessed such scenes since the Vietnam War protests of 1968. It was a sea of placards, a cacophony of megaphones, as we alighted from the coach into the throng. We were then swept along past high-end boutiques and commercial art galleries onto Piccadilly and past the Ritz. I spotted Bill holding up one end of a banner, he had a smile on his face for the first time since the rent rises were announced. He might yet be spared camping on Shoreditch Green.

I was running through the crowd to capture the occasion on my camera, stopping to chat with comrades past and present, and others I'd yet to know but would be working with in the coming months and years. Turning into Whitehall, Dan, Lyndsay, and Lindsey led the way with Russell – it felt like an unstoppable force. Lyndsey stood atop the wall facing No10 and made her speech. 'We're here to tell David Cameron, Boris Johnson and everyone else in a position of power the residents of the New Era Estate do not intend on leaving their homes.' Then through the gates they went to deliver the petition to David Cameron at No10. Diane

Abbott, MP for neighbouring Hackney North was spotted trying to sneak in at the back and politely sent packing.

The campaign had been a huge success. It had become a global story, a lightning rod for the wider issue of London's chronic housing crisis. 'New Era for All' had become a rallying cry for housing campaigns across the Capital.

The week before Christmas Westbrook announced that they had sold the estate to a housing association – Dolphin Living. The estate had been saved. The news not only inspired relief and jubilation in Hoxton but it gave hope to others that there could be no lost causes now. Everybody could fight back – as long as you stuck together.

CHAPTER 4

SAVE SOHO –
THE HEART OF LONDON

A mong the social media blizzard kicked up by the New Era campaign was a call for support to 'Save Soho'. At first it seemed improbable that one of the historic heartlands of the West End should be facing any kind of serious existential threat but I decided to meet Save Soho founder Tim Arnold for a stroll around the area to survey the scene and shoot a video to promote the cause. We agreed to rendezvous outside the 12 Bar Club in Denmark Street, not strictly part of Soho being on the other side of Charing Cross Road but its status as the street of music was key to the story of what was happening.

Tim Arnold was an incredible force of nature as both an activist and musician. His Soho concept album saw a 'time travelling character' the Soho Hobo traversing centuries of the area's history in song. His personal history was intimately tied to the zone. He'd been signed to Sony in the '90s with his Britpop band Jocasta, gigging at the 12 Bar Club and the Astoria over the road. After the band split, he kept pumping out quality music across 23 albums, collaborating with legends such as Iggy Pop and Lindsay Kemp. Save Soho was a personal mission as well as a community campaign.

Waiting for Tim, Denmark Street was clogged with traffic on a midweek morning. Buses and tipper trucks on diversion from the Tottenham Court Road Crossrail works formed a convoy of woe. This narrow ancient thoroughfare was dwarfed by the double-deckers bumper-to-bumper with heavy goods vehicles. This is where the earliest cases of the bubonic plague outbreak were reported in 1665, with 1300 of the dead being laid to rest in St Giles' churchyard situated at the end of the street. Camden council's Denmark Street Conservation Area Appraisal and Management Strategy from 2010 notes, 'The whole of the Denmark Street Conservation Area lies within an Area of Archaeological Priority. It has been identified by English Heritage Greater London Archaeological Advisory Service as the suburbs of Roman Londinium, part of Saxon Lundenwic and an area of extensive medieval and post medieval settlement.' The area's historic significance doesn't appear to provide a sufficient impediment to the rapacious development that could eventually ravage the area more thoroughly than the plague.

People carrying instruments in cases ducked into the surviving music shops. Among the roster was Angel Music / Vintage and Quality / Second Hand Guitars Upstairs. A shop window sign told how Old Sax had moved further north out of the area. Wunjo Keys. Wunjo Guitars. Hanks. Enterprise Studios were having a Clearance Sale of 'Drum Kits, Cabs, Heads ... and Much More'. A bloke stopped to light up a fag outside Regent Sounds Studio where Mick and Keith probably lit up before going inside to lay down some of the early Rolling Stones tracks. A No 29 bus trundled to a standstill at the lights pumping out a heavy metal of the diesel engine variety. Behind it the row of late 17th century buildings that formed part of the original development of the 1680s looked in fine form. No 6 was where the Sex Pistols lived and rehearsed, the graffiti they left behind on the walls later being preserved in a very un-punk act of heritage that doesn't extend to the growing list of music businesses being forced out of Tin Pan Alley.

Renzo Piano's enormous primary coloured carbuncle, Central St. Giles, dominates one end of the street as if it has decided to attempt to obliterate the psychogeographical legacy of Queen Matilda's 12th century leper hospital and the notorious 18th century Rookeries of Hogarth's Gin Lane through sheer weight of glass and steel. All it does is simply reinforce the bad vibes of the area, intensify the winds that howl through its open walkways into the bleak courtyard starved of natural light.

The spirit of place was so strong that the mighty techno wizards of Google relocated to Kings Cross, aligning with William Blake's vision of Jerusalem rising from the fields beneath Islington. Rock'n'roll, blues, jazz and folk feed off this energy and yet it's the music that's being forced to move on, dispersed around the capital and beyond.

A Blue Plaque on No 9 Denmark Street records that 'This street was "Tin Pan Alley" 1911-1992. Home of the British Publishers and Songwriters and their meeting place The Giaconda.' Yet another double-decker bus swept past and I expected to find the plaque missing when it'd departed.

A steady stream of pedestrians moved between St Giles and Charing Cross Road, wannabe rock stars stood and gazed at the vintage guitars in the window, rosewood semi-acoustic Gibsons so polished they reflected the clippety-clop office workers passing by. I even contemplated a midlife crisis purchase of a 12-string Rickenbacker that I'd dreamed about since I was 15.

The top end of Charing Cross Road was carnage. Guys in hard hats and fluorescent orange jackets blocked the street and waved out trucks from what used to be the site of the legendary Astoria Theatre – now levelled to the ground to make way for Crossrail.

I saw my first London gig there – The Mission in 1987. The fountains beneath Centre Point where we loitered before the show surrounded by patchouli drenched goths swilling Pink Lady have also gone. West End Extra reported that after a time being stashed away in a Wembley car park the fountains have found a new home in the grounds of Hooke Park, Dorset.

A bright orange crane slowly swung across Charing Cross Road in synchronicity with the pigeons swooping down from the window ledges of Shaldon Mansions. This grand red-brick block of apartments was a vestige of a previous incursion on Denmark Street in 1887 when the Metropolitan Board of Works decided to widen and extend the old Crown Street to aid the flow of traffic to the new Charing Cross station, chopping off the western end of Denmark Street in the process. Shaldon Mansions was built by the developer James Hartnoll whose similar blocks along Rosebery Avenue and Grays Inn Road all bear the names of places in Devon. A helpful commentator on my blog post about this curiosity pointed out that Hartnoll's family originated from Devon although he'd been born into poverty in Southwark. In the time before council dwellings, Hartnoll was a significant builder of flats for working people across London. In common with the latest assault on St Giles, the new buildings of the 1880s were met with criticism, complaints about their 'elevations of imposing height' and their 'showiness'. The notice posted in the London Gazette announcing Hartnoll's death on the 23rd January 1900 gave one of his addresses as Halberstadt Mansions (the original name of Shaldon Mansions). A number of street names in London were changed during the First World War due to strong anti-German sentiment – the Royal Family even changed their surname from Saxe-Coburg and Gotha to Windsor – so it's possible that Halberstadt, a town in Saxony, became Shaldon Mansions for the same reason.

Returning to Denmark Street, Tim Arnold was stood outside the 12 Bar Club looking like a rock star dressed all in black and wearing sunglasses on a grey January day. The 12 Bar Club had posters in the window for the Grand Opening Weekend of its new premises on Holloway Road in a couple of weeks time featuring King Kurt. It turned out to be a short-lived move.

As we were shooting the intro to the video a young man emerged from the 12 Bar and lit up a fag. I asked him about the situation at the club and he told us it was closing that very day. As we spoke containers of kit were being wheeled out of the venue into a removal van. The cause of the closure he tells us was development around the CrossRail project. By the time of completion the trail of loss left behind by CrossRail will be so great that you'll be able to move from one side of Greater London to the other with little reason to stop off in between, the gigantic Crossrail tunnel hollowing out the heart of London as it burrows through its core.

He told us a group of developers owned a lot of the property in the street and the 12 Bar was one of the first victims. The reaction from regulars and staff ranged from sadness, disbelief and anger to indifference from some, just more change, time to move on to the next scene, wherever that was.

The 12 Bar had been there since 1992, he went on, it was a folk club before that. The roster of famous names to have graced its modest stage early in their careers included Adele, Keane were discovered there, Jeff Buckley, James Blunt. For Tim Arnold this was where every album he'd released had been road-tested. Young independent artists depended on venues like the 12 Bar, he said.

The kit from the Club was being loaded into a removal van by the kerb – a poignant moment as the vital organs were removed. Denmark Street is another victim of London's rapidly changing landscape. The historic home of London's music business being slowly dismantled behind the facade of the remaining music shops as the tourists and the buses trundle past. Tim said you got kids coming to buy their first guitar or do their first gig and you may even see Eric Clapton or Jimmy Paige looking in the shops to 'see if they can find a guitar they used in the '60s'. The fear, he told me, is that the area will be transformed into something that feels like an airport lounge.

Carlo, one of the owners of the 12 Bar, came out onto the pavement from the alley beside Hanks guitar shop, to watch the PA being loaded into the van. He greeted Tim with a big warm smile. He seemed quietly resigned to what was happening and told us how Transport for London cleared the site for the owners, and this is the natural progression to revamp the area. The building is at least Georgian he said. The music venue started in 1993/4 as The Forge, opened as a room for jam sessions for music shop and rehearsal room staff. It soon became 'Internationally known', he said with a glow of pride. 'That's life, things happen', Carlo said philosophically. He was told in 1997 they had one or two years, so he's happy to have lasted so long. I asked him about his favourite memories. 'Drinking too much wine', he laughed.

A stack of drums went into the van as Carlo and Tim chatted on the pavement, the church of St Giles in the Fields behind. Tim asked if they'd stay in the West End, 'Of course' he would but the rents were too high. Soho was now a place of 'prestige premises' Carlo said, the developers preferred bigger companies.

We stood outside Regent Sounds where the Rolling Stones recorded, ghosts of music past wafted amongst the crowds. There were plans to incorporate the music heritage into the redevelopment: a Jagger room in the boutique hotel, an app showing you where Rod Stewart picked his nose. A musician standing in the doorway of Regent Sounds on a break in his session told us that acid jazz was born in this street. 'This is a micro village of musicians, to turn it into a tourist attraction would be a sad loss', Tim told me. He bought his first guitar here. The thought of it becoming an amusement park made him wince. Camden council claimed on their website that this was one of the six most unique streets in London. This felt more like a pitch to developers rather than a commitment to protect the heritage. Save Soho was working with the landlords and the politicians to try and preserve the venues that survived in the area before it was too late.

This clustering of musical talents in one street will be scattered far and wide. Slowly creative minds are fleeing London. Once dislodged from well-established perches with artistic communities broken up, the instrument makers, artists, designers, writers, actors, directors, craftspeople looking for a new home drift off to Thanet, Berlin, Birmingham maybe with a temporary stop-over in Barking with the developers breathing down their necks. Once, priced out of West and North London, the bohemians headed East, but there is nowhere East left to go this side of Kreuzburg.

A man overheard us in the street and stopped to talk. This was a fella called Andrew Ellis and he told us he used to work in No 6 for a sleeve design agency called Hipgnosis who did all the famous sleeves for Pink Floyd, Led Zeppelin, Paul McCartney – 'they were the guys who floated the pig over Battersea Power Station. They did Dark Side of the Moon.' The Sex Pistols used to rehearse behind their studio: 'Glen Matlock lived in the flat upstairs'. He listed the legendary musicians who passed up and down the narrow Georgian staircase – Peter Gabriel, Paul McCartney, Led Zepellin. Zenos Greek Book Shop was on the ground floor. I asked him if we were in danger of losing the essence of Soho. 'We're in danger of losing the essence of London', he replied earnestly, all the 'cultural hotspots' could be wiped away by developers.

Back on Charing Cross Road we surveyed the wreckage of the Astoria where Tim played in the '90s with Baby Bird who had a huge hit with You're Gorgeous. He pointed out that two more smaller venues – LA2 and Mean Fiddler – were also demolished: three venues wiped out for the sake of another entrance to the Elizabeth Line.

We crossed the road and ducked down Manette Street beside the old Foyles Building. Tim stopped outside the Borderline, a venue whose future seems secure. It was a gig here with his first band Jocasta that led to Tim being signed to Sony Records, a huge moment in a musician's life. These are the kinds of venues that breed legends. Manette Street itself is a street of stories. Originally named Rose Street it was changed in honour of Dr Manette, a character in Charles Dickens' novel A Tale of Two Cities who lived here in the book. In the late 1800s it also gained fame as a street of anarchists and radicals, providing a home to political refugees and exiles from the continent.

Moving through into Soho proper, crossing the border between the borough of Camden into the City of Westminster, we came to Jazz After Dark on Greek Street. Tim highlighted this as the kind of venue that once thrived in Soho and is now an endangered rarity in need of protection. It's where Amy Winehouse performed on numerous occasions – she's commemorated on the menu with the Back to Black cocktail and Amy's Platter.

Our last stop took us to one of the great surviving deposits of Soho's live music lore. Tim put in a call to Sweetie at the St Moritz and he agreed to meet as the lunchtime rush started to die down. We moved laterally across the Soho street grid as the bustle of daytime Soho moved on around us. Production houses, advertising and film companies still occupy some of the old Georgian and Victorian buildings, but change is creeping through the area block by block. You hear of edit houses moving east in search of more favourable rents and larger premises. The old ghosts of Blake, Stukeley, Marx, and Bacon still walk abroad at night unseen amongst the late night pavement drinkers, but even they may soon be forced to find new haunts.

You could easily miss the narrow doorway at 159 Wardour Street. Tim skipped through the Soho traffic and out of view. A sign on the wall read 'St Moritz Club – Still Rocking' with a drawing of jagged alpine peaks. Inside was not the rock'n'roll mecca I'd imagined but a mock Alpine chalet serving up fine Swiss food. The last pairs of diners delved into their fondue as Sweetie in his chef's whites emerged from the kitchen wiping his hands to greet us. Aged 77, Sweetie had just finished cooking the lunchtime service. He had a bright round face illuminated by a cherubic smile, an accent difficult to place, a bustling energy as he led us through the restaurant to the entrance to the club. He told us how his name came from working as a pastry cook at Madame Floris in the 1960s. The restaurant opened mostly for au pair girls and students who also came for his cakes and called him Sweetie. At no point did I hear anyone call him by any other name.

Down in the darkened basement club, which lies below the restaurant, Sweetie recounted how he started hosting live music in 1963-4. He listed some of the famous musicians to have graced the tiny stage set into one end of the low arched ceiling basement. There was Delroy Williams and the Raisins, Joe Strummer played there with the 101ers and wrote a song about Sweetie – Sweetie in the St Moritz, a tune I still can't shake from my head. Episode 6 did a weekly residence before they changed their name and became Deep Purple. Jimi Hendrix used to drink in the St Moritz after playing at the Marquee. Sweetie smiled and told us how many of the musicians from the Marquee used to drink there: Lemmy, Iron

Maiden, Duran Duran and many more, everybody passed through this basement club at some point.

The gigs were almost nightly. Tim called it the last basement club in Soho open to all artists, exactly what Save Soho was trying to protect, 'an all inclusive Soho', and he hoped new venues would spawn from the legends born at venues like the St Mortiz.

Sweetie had been in Soho since 1958, I asked him how Soho had changed. 'All these companies are buying it all up', he told us, 'Back in the old days all the restaurants knew each other, they were small operations, that's changed. The big companies moving into Soho are making it harder for the smaller venues to survive and thrive. Once there were loads of little clubs', he said with passion, 'Les Cousins, they used to have folk music in the basement'. Wikipedia mentions that artists such as Bert Jansch, John Martyn, Sandy Denny, Paul Simon and John Renbourn played significant gigs there early in their careers along with a Who's Who list of folk musicians and bands. 'Infant Terrible was another one' he said. 'We are losing the character of Soho, people are coming to live in Soho and are complaining about the noise. Don't come to live in Soho if you want a quiet life.'

———

A week later I was back at the 12 Bar on my way to see Tim Arnold play the St Moritz. A coalition of activists had occupied the site, most prominently a group called the Soho Bohemians. The place was packed, dimly lit by a row of dangling lamps. A bloke thrashed out blues-folk guitar while another spat and howled through a harmonica. It was like a staged reconstruction of 1960s Greenwich Village.

There were faces in the crowd who I'd meet again over the coming years of occupations and actions elsewhere across London. I didn't realise it at the time, but the occupation of 12 Bar became a mustering point of the resistance against the assault on the soul of London. Outside I chatted with Bianca holding up a sign that read 'Save the Spirit of Soho'. She referred to the lively scene inside as a 'community meeting', a reclamation of the space for the artists and musicians of Soho. They wanted to 'keep Soho sleazy', she said, the sex workers and small traders were all being forced out, they were fighting to save 'the character and culture of Soho – the grittiness'.

Spotting my camera a fella came across to introduce himself, Henry Scott-Irvine from the Save Denmark Street campaign. He led me into the narrow passageway that ran behind the 12 Bar, the sound of the anguished blues-folk singer spilling out through the ancient brickwork. The alleyway was sheathed in scaffolding and wooden panels while the developers erased a small section of the map that had been in the London street plan since the late Middle Ages, hoping to hide their crime behind a hoarding.

'This was a thriving hub of activity', Scott-Irvine declared, pointing to where there was once a tattoo parlour, Enterprise re-hearsal studios, and the doors to the 17th century Old Forge where the folk singer assaulted his battered guitar. Henry called Denmark Street 'the street of music' which 'started in 1911 with Wright's publishing empire'. He explained the through-line that took us to the original offices of the NME in Denmark Street where in the 1950s they created the first singles chart. He told of how Larry Parnes had his offices here and gave birth to British rock'n'roll by signing Tommy Steele and Marty Wilde shortly followed by Billy Fury. Then came the guitar shops and recording studios includ-ing the legendary Regent Sound Studios where the Rolling Stones recorded their debut album across five days in early 1964. 'Pete Townsend had an account at Macari's (guitar shop) because he trashed so many guitars', Henry continued. The plan, he said, is to turn all the offices above the music shops into apartments and boutique hotels. 'Tin Pan Alley is unique in the world. Don't let the music die in Denmark Street.'

I went back inside the 12 Bar where my mate Andy was feeding crisps to a pack of hungry dogs. Me and Andy shared a room in Forest Gate when I moved to London as an 18-year-old student, initially bonding over our love of music, knocking out what we thought of as songs on our guitars, recording them on borrowed 4-tracks. Andy is still making music, he's really quite good now, but he'll never get the chance to play the 12 Bar Club.

We got chatting to one of the musicians who'd just been up on the stage. Craig worked at Enterprise Studios and spent many evenings jamming and playing at the 12 Bar. It was 'something special' to play here one last time he said. 'This is Ground Zero for music in the UK' he said, 'music is our cultural heritage', and its spiritual and geographical heart was under attack. Craig has seen musicians being forced out of the capital by the spread of gentrification, and now it has reached the epicentre of the music community. You get the sense from talking to Craig just how high the stakes are for the community of musicians in London. The fight to save Denmark Street started to feel like a last stand of sorts.

There was something uplifting about the scene at the 12 Bar: even though the club was doomed, the week or so of lively 'community meetings' gave it a decent send off. Leaving the 12 Bar I retraced my steps of the trail the week before, along Denmark Street through Soho to the St Moritz where we arrived in time to see Tim Arnold take the stage. Music was alive in Soho and Tin Pan Alley for now.

———

It was a year before I returned for a proper look at what was happening in Denmark Street, this time in the company of Henry Scott-Irvine. I emerged from the new Tottenham Court Road station to be confronted by the diggers excavating the heart of Denmark Place and dumping it in a huge pile. The route round to Denmark Street was via a series of wood panelled walkways to shield intrepid pedestrians from the construction work. The final passage was along a metal mesh channel where the sound of jackhammers rattled the fillings in your teeth. Several double-decker buses on diversion lined 'the street of music' bumper-to-bumper, engines pumping out particulates. Even the immortal Keith Richards would have struggled in this noxious environment if he returned for a visit to Regent Sounds. A cement mixer and fully-laden dumper truck joined the traffic queue obscuring the Georgian buildings on the other side of the road. Denmark Street was being choked into submission.

I found Henry looking in the window of Macari's guitar shop (est.1958) next to the boarded up site of the 12-Bar. He gave me a brief overview of the current state-of-play at that point in 2016, where the guitar shops had been told they would be offered new leases when current ones expired, meaning that at street level music was still apparent, but in the offices above the shops nearly all the music businesses had left – the agents, managers, guitar makers, recording studios. 'There were at least six guitar makers in the street, now there is only one.' Henry told me he's campaigning to bring a guitar-making school to the street to revive the craft in the area. This seemed ever more pressing as I'd filmed a protest against the last guitar making degree in the country being closed down at my old alma mater, London Metropolitan University. The assault on the city's musical heritage was coming from all sides.

We moved down into the alleyway between Hanks Guitar Shop and the 12 Bar where I first spoke to Henry that night of the occupation. The alley that ran behind the 12 Bar into Denmark Place was blocked off, rubble piled up along by the wall, but one poignant relic remained. On the wall was a black board punctured all over with staples trapping the ripped corners of adverts for band members that once covered this patch of the alley. Session musicians looking for work, bands seeking musicians, drummers and guitarists searching for bands, all came to stand in this spot and gaze at this notice board. This was the only thing left in the alleyway after the venue closed, the rehearsal studios boarded up. Only one scrap of paper survived, a sticker that someone had tried to rip off: 'Laranja – Indie vibes from Birmingham – download new single Sweet for free'.

Across the street the lunchtime bells of St Giles Church rang out. Office workers passed along Denmark Street towards Charing Cross Road in the daily hunt for food. The traffic still idled in a barely moving marmalade of woe.

Centre Point loomed over the whole scene, a 1960s folly that should have served as a warning to future developers. Beneath it lies the rubble of what was Denmark Place and Henry told me the patch of cleared ground will spawn the Now Building, some sort of internet shopping experience in physical form. The lines of slowly moving traffic and shoppers on foot moved through the chaos like a column of refugees fleeing a disaster area.

Henry looked on with sadness and anger at the loss of London's precious music heritage to be replaced with what he feared would be a 'corporate hell'. But he refused to give up the fight. Henry and the Save Tin Pan Alley campaign continued their guerrilla war against the developers. And the last time I checked, the remaining music shops hang on in Denmark Street, still supplying the guitar heroes of the past and the dreamers of tomorrow.

CHAPTER 5

VIVA SWEETSTOPIA - THE NORTH LONDON INDEPENDENT MICROSTATE

After the triumph of the residents of the New Era Estate, activists, the public and press alike scoured the map for the next battleground, the likely scene of a David and Goliath clash of residents versus greedy developers. One of the groups fighting valiantly to save their community was Barnet Housing Action, whom I'd met when making a video about Barnet council's scandalous treatment of residents on the West Hendon Estate. The council had partnered with Barratt Homes to develop the estate, leading to the decanting of non-secure tenants to other estates earmarked for regeneration, with secure tenants moved away from properties in the prime waterside locations to a new block beside the dual carriageway. Leaseholders I'd spoken to, who'd bought their council flats under Thatcher's 'Right to Buy' policy, had been offered a fraction of the market value of their homes, barely enough to purchase a share in the part-buy / part-rent properties in the new West Hendon Waterside development. It beggared belief that such a scheme was legal. Not only was it legal but it was being repeated across the city.

Barnet Housing Action now alerted me to evictions taking place on the Sweets Way Estate in Totteridge & Whetstone, North London. Annington Homes and Barnet council were in the process of evicting around 140 families in order to demolish perfectly good houses and build a 'luxury development'. Housing had become the lightning rod issue, and after his high-profile involvement in the New Era campaign, Russell Brand was being seen as a conduit for this energy. He reacted to the Sweets Way situation in the usual measured, understated way – by issuing a global call to action for a 'Sweets Way Sleepover' and turning up to the start of the ensuing occupation in an ice cream van.

Despite the housing crisis being in the news daily, the situation at Sweets Way had barely been mentioned in the press. A brutal wave of evictions had been underway for weeks with long-term tenants turfed out onto the streets, possessions in bin-liners, and shunted off to temporary accommodation. The hope was that Russell's celebrity and free Mr Whippy would raise the profile of the plight of the Sweets Way residents, and then who knows.

It was a cold, wet March midweek night near the end of the Northern Line. I turned the corner into the swirl of tree-lined roads of neat 1980s houses that made up the Sweets Way Estate. Would anyone venture this far out towards the London fringe, I wondered? A small group in activist drag stood around burning logs on an improvised brazier. A disco light strobed against a wooden fence. I spotted a couple of faces I vaguely recognised from the occupation of the 12 Bar. Then the shrill peal of an ice cream van blaring out O Sole Mio came across the rooftops and stopped outside the house. Russell appeared through the service window and started dishing out free Mr Whippys. The estate kids snaked through the legs of Brand fans to get to the front of the scrum. Videographers from the Guardian and Vice and a myriad of media outlets suddenly illuminated the scene with their lights. A German TV crew found themselves stranded at the back of the throng. It was another bizarre movie scene being played out with a Hollywood actor on a London housing estate, real-life neo-realism directed through the ether by Fellini or Antonioni – activism as spectacle. It made more sense experienced through a lens watched on the camera screen rather than in the flesh when I looked up to check if it was real.

With Mr Whippy dripping down his hand Russell addressed the crowd talking about the 'corporate creep' eroding and displacing communities. He talked about the opportunity to participate in a new movement, and had some ice cream. Would this become the salute of the new nascent movement, an ice cream cone raised in defiance starting to melt?

From somewhere in the back of the van Jasmine Stone from Focus E15 appeared to give a speech linking the Focus E15 campaign to the situation on Sweets Way and a pattern of redevelopment and council estate evictions sweeping across London. Since the Carpenters Estate occupation, Jasmine had become something of a minor celebrity on the activist circuit, a young mum thrust into the limelight in this city of conflict. A teenage resident of the estate then called out the chant from the ice cream van that was taken up by the assembled throng, 'Repopulate the Sweets Way Estate, Repopulate the Sweets Way Estate'. A bearded activist took the mic on the lawn near the disco light. I became too distracted by the half-eaten ice cream in his other hand and the gloops of soft serve clinging to his beard to properly listen to what he was saying and instead joined the stream of people moving towards the free food being given out by the Hare Krishnas. It felt surreal at the time but looks even more bizarre reviewing the footage these few years later as if it belongs to a different era altogether.

We struggled through the now large crowd into the house chosen for the sleepover. Russell had become a Pied Piper figure with a cluster of the local kids hanging off his clothing, cameras looming, including my own. In the lounge, a fella was sat on the sofa playing old Turkish songs on a violin and singing along. As we slumped into one of the bedrooms we attempted to reflect on the craziness of the scene, especially for me having grown up in a council house like this one, in a bedroom just like the one now full to the brim with media. Russell, at this time more at ease in front of a lens than away from it, lapsed into casual conversation with me about the Sweets Way campaign and the housing struggle in general, whilst behind me, a bank of journalists was recording every word. He was conducting a press conference in a bare bedroom of a council house condemned for demolition surrounded by a posse of children that formed a juvenile praetorian guard.

I went back downstairs. The violinist now played the rousing Italian anti-fascist folk tune Bella Ciao, singing the verses in Turkish with the attendant gathering singing along. In an adjacent room I met former resident Esma and her two teenage children. They found a home on Sweets Way after ten years in temporary accommodation and lived there happily for five years before being told by Barnet council that they had to leave. The council hadn't informed them of the consequences of turning down the alternative accommodation offered (some people were removed from the list for turning down one property, others had eight choices). They consequently found themselves being notified they were being moved into emergency accommodation the night before the move. Any items they couldn't take with them they were instructed by the council to sell. Within a day they had been wrenched from their home in Sweets Way and placed in emergency accommodation in a neighbouring borough, in a house with a front door that wouldn't lock. They told me of the shock, of how unexpected it all was: after all, the homes on Sweets Way are in perfect condition, they said. The eldest child was doing his GCSEs at the time and both kids now faced a 90-minute journey to school each day taking in three buses from the temporary accommodation they'd been placed in that had no hot water. 'They've made our life a misery', said the 13-year-old girl when I asked what they thought of Barnet council. 'They say they're bringing families together but actually, they're dividing families.'

This kind of treatment sounded like the clearance of communities by occupying forces during a time of war: officials coming during the night, ordering people to pack what they could carry and leave. The insecurity and brutality of forced relocation away from community and friends. On the evidence of what I witnessed on Sweets Way and at West Hendon this appeared to be a deliberate and systematic move by Barnet council to replace lower-income council tenants with wealthier private residents.

For Esma and her children, the Sleepover was a form of homecoming, however brief, and the hope that perhaps the tide could be turned. Outside people were starting to make plans for the night, most had no intention of sleeping but were engaged in intense conversation. I spoke to people who'd travelled from Southampton and Coventry, some intending to stay on till the bitter end of the campaign. Amongst this clan of the committed, I met Daniel, one of those faces I'd recognised from the 12 Bar. Daniel was livestreaming from beside the brazier and drew me into his broadcast. A committed activist of previous occupations elsewhere across London, Daniel was in for the long haul and before I headed out beyond the glow of the bonfires he invited me to return once they'd settled in. As I was leaving, the call went out over the loud hailer to take up residence in some of the empty houses. I traipsed back to Leytonstone on the tube processing what I'd just witnessed.

I returned to Sweets Way in the summer four months later, meeting Liam on one of the verdant green spaces that wound through the estate. Originally built as housing for military families, Sweets Way had been designed for life, sympathetic to the contours of the environment formed by the meandering Dollis Brook, mindful of its place at the foot of the south Hertfordshire uplands. There's a fringe belief that the true location of Camelot (or the inspiration for the Norman mythologists) was nearby at Camlet Moat in what was now Trent Park. Liam and his cohorts were rebuilding a form of Camelot here on the Sweets Way Estate, an attempted beacon of hope, an alternative reality for Sweets Way and the many other estates earmarked for 'regeneration'.

All the houses now had brown metal shutters on the doors and windows. Liam told me how the contractors had been smashing up the houses in a deliberate blighting of the estate prior to demolition. The 'Show Home' they were renovating with volunteers sat alongside one of the recently blighted houses to demonstrate the before and after.

Donated building materials were piled up outside the house under unofficial renovation – sheets of plasterboard, a new toilet. Kids used a heavy-duty trolley to give each other rides on the patio. We stepped inside one of the houses wrecked by the new owners Annington Homes, houses that just a few months ago had been cherished family abodes before the evictions and relocations. Valuable items such as copper piping had been ripped out by Annington, but also the plastic waste pipes from the sinks to prevent re-occupation – an even more senseless destruction in the context of London's chronic housing crisis. Liam showed me sinks and toilets smashed by the developers, and pointed out the perversity of paying people to destroy liveable houses to make them impossible to live in. The wreckage of shattered sinks littered rooms that once housed families. Lampshades lay on the floor, a broken toilet dumped in a bedroom – an unnecessary act of wanton vandalism in pursuit of profit. It was bizarre. Standing in a bedroom, recently somebody's home, I thought of Esma and her children in the inadequate temporary accommodation they'd been shunted into, and it seemed even more scandalous and illogical – criminal in fact.

Liam explained how this was Ministry of Defence land until the MOD sold off its housing stock to Annington for £1.67 billion in 1996, who then leased it back to the government. The National Audit Office disclosed in 2018 that the government had lost up to £4.2 billion through the deal. The Guardian reported how the privatisation of military housing was being viewed as a disastrous move. Most recently, the estate had been leased to Notting Hill Housing Trust as social housing, during which time a new community had formed. The evictions started as soon as Barnet council granted Annington planning permission for the site.

The carpet had been ripped off the stairs that Liam led me up, a pile of broken tiles was scattered across the landing. What had been the kitchen had debris strewn across the floor and a section of wall from another room propped up to the side. None of this made any sense. These were not derelict houses, this was not a brownfield site but a thriving community, a public asset dispensed with in a bad deal, now being laid to waste with the families dispersed to hostels and temporary accommodation while their former homes were ripped apart.

In the adjacent house, the signs of renovation and rebuilding were evident ahead of the grand opening of the Show Home. A sign on the patio door warned of wet paint. A new toilet and floor tiles waited outside to be installed. Carved into the floorboards were the words:

FIRST THEY IGNORE YOU
THEN THEY LAUGH AT YOU

THEN THEY FIGHT YOU
THEN YOU WIN

The sound of hammering came from a downstairs bathroom where a woman, Anna, with her young daughter was hammering sawn up floorboards to the wall as part of her idea for a 'rustic bathroom'. Once this was done, she told me, she'd fix the plumbing.

Anna explained why she was doing the work. 'We need to prove that the community can do something, and I think it's important to have a house for people instead of a house for profit, and with a little help from local companies we can achieve great houses for a great community and unfortunately people who are in charge need a reminder of that, that to create something amazing you need great spirit in the community and that is not going to happen if you're going to have private developers selling houses for millions of pounds and making a profit off them.'

Anna used to live on the estate for over five and a half years with her two children and they were given notice to move out. As a single parent, it was difficult. She described the estate as 'one big family'. London was in danger of becoming a 'ghost town' she says. The city needs a working class in her opinion, and you need houses for the working classes. 'The houses should be for people to create homes not for investors to create profit.'

Liam was working out the second half of the kitchen floor. One half had been laid with reclaimed slate roofing from an abandoned factory taken with the permission of the owner. The house was due to open to the public and media the next day. Word had been going out on Twitter. A half-laid kitchen floor just wouldn't do. Liam sized up the remaining bare patch and glanced at the stack of slates. This revolution would be built on the foundation of home improvements rather than convoluted polemics.

This Show Home was to demonstrate what could be done with a

house in a few days with little resources aside from donated, recy-cled and re-used materials. The residents and activists were undo-ing the damage done by Annington Homes, and hopefully sending out a powerful message of what communities could achieve with minimal support. They wanted to show that this would be possible anywhere – communities could regenerate their own estates, and dispel the myth of unaffordable estate regeneration. There'd been a pattern across the city of tenants being decanted from estates to allow for essential regeneration works only then to be told that a portion, or a whole estate, in the case of the Balfron Tower, would have to be sold to cover the costs.

Liam stopped talking while a van full of police drove past. What they really wanted to get across was what Liam called 'the racket of the regeneration industry that we see playing out all across London – private companies are making immense profits off of public hous-ing stock and this is one example,' he explained. He continued that the rationale used when selling off public housing was that there was no alternative, that the public sector can't afford to bring the homes up to a liveable standard. The community regeneration of Sweets Way was a riposte to that idea. It would take minimal resources to allow residents to regenerate their own homes. It was an inspiring and uplifting project, undoing Annington's blight of the estate.

Across the car park, I approached a different world: the independ-ent microstate of Sweetstopia. I'd forgotten to bring my passport so wasn't sure if I'd be allowed to cross the barricaded entrance that sealed off the two corner houses that compromised London's latest autonomous community.

The border wall was decorated with brightly painted slogans –
'Get A Job', 'Barricade and Resist', 'Resist + Reclaim', 'M11 Crew'.
A chair was placed beside the gate I guess in case visitors had to
wait for entry. Seeing 'M11 Crew' daubed at the entrance brought
to mind another of London's independent microstates – two in fact.
Wanstonia and Leytonstonia were declared during the protracted
campaign to stop the building of the M11 Link Road in the early
'90s destroying hundreds of homes and trees running through the
heart of Leyton, Leytonstone and Wanstead. The streets earmarked
for demolition had become home to Europe's largest community
of artists, many of the houses themselves had been transformed
into artworks. I interviewed one of the key protagonists, Ian Bourn,
in our local pub for my book, This Other London. He told me of
the foundation of Leytonstonia and the long discussions that took
place over what to use as currency, with the carrot eventually being adopted. In December 2018 people gathered on George Green,
Wanstead to remember the ancient oak tree that became one of the
flashpoints and the heart of Wanstonia. The memory of the protest, the occupation, the resistance, was etched into the collective

psyche of the area – Leytonstonia and Wanstonia live on. And here the M11 Crew had re-emerged in a remote corner of North London 25 years later.

I was granted entry to Sweetstopia with minimal formality at the border by Daniel, a face from the 12 Bar occupation and again illuminated by the flickering flames of the brazier at the Sleepover in March. I was immediately greeted by the wonderful aroma of lavender wafting through the air from a bonfire in the far corner. The first slogan I saw inside read 'Trew World Order' a reference to Russell's YouTube show The Trews and a slogan that would be repurposed later that year in very different surroundings for his arena tour of South Africa, Australia and New Zealand.

A homemade wooden framed greenhouse growing cucumbers, potatoes, tomatoes, strawberries and peppers stood on the concrete forecourt – an early sign of the utopia being constructed amongst the debris of demolition. Steph and Vegas talked me through their permaculture allotment laid out on the concrete paving slabs in a variety of re-purposed growing containers. Vegas was picking some salad leaves to go in a sandwich made with donated bread. Steph showed me the tomatoes, lettuce, cucumbers, courgettes, spinach and beans growing from an assortment of car tyres and plant pots. Sinks and bathtubs rescued from the blighted houses now sprouted healthy crops of vegetables, salads, and greens. There was a patch of tomatoes and beans growing where a missing paving slab had exposed the earth. The image of food sprouting from the concrete was a great symbol of what the Sweetstopians were creating. Steph offered up a sprig of pungent fresh mint to my nose. She then pointed out beetroot and chard and more herbs, beans and salad.

The fella burning the lavender handed Steph a bag of nettles to make either tea or compost. Discarded pallets had been converted into upright planters. An old ladder had become another series of brightly painted tubs sprouting rosemary and other herbs.

Reclaimed panes of double-glazing topped wooden beds made from foraged shed wood to make glasshouses. The fallout of the organised vandalism of the developers on the other side of the border had helped build a permaculture arcadia in Sweetstopia. It would be an impressive display of gardening in any context, worthy of a medal at Chelsea Flower Show.

Vegas approached with a box of seeds that had just been donated. A local health food shop donated leftover food at the end of each day. There was evidently a strong sense of goodwill towards both new communities that had taken root on Sweets Way since that night in March. Vegas then proceeded to procure a packet of crisps to go with her freshly picked salad sandwich.

Steph showed me how they use half-broken eggshells as seed planters explaining how permaculture was centred around re-using what we had rather than buying new stuff. It made me think of the 1990s slogan 'Resistance was fertile' from the guerrilla gardeners who sowed marijuana plants on Parliament Square during a protest that successfully grew at the foot of the statue of Winston Churchill.

There were around 15-20 inhabitants of Sweetstopia spread across several houses within the barricaded enclosure. Steph said that if they could safely access the back gardens, they could grow all the food they needed. But with the bailiffs circling the backs of the houses, they had to remain boarded up with the central enclosure the effective heart of the microstate. It was like a miniature walled city.

Daniel explained how Sweetstopia started shortly after that night when they came to help the families with just a small group of activists which had since grown. Phase one, he said, was to repair the damage done by the contractors: squatters had renovated more houses on the estate that had been vandalised by the builders and 'some of them are works of art'.

He believed the next level of the housing struggle was about 'sustainability and autonomy – how to reclaim your whole community as a little self-governing unit.

It's kind of a game but a very serious game, it isn't a joke even if it sounds like it.' and he pointed to the concrete walls and the barricades. 'Occupy Everywhere' was painted on a discarded door propped up against the outside of the house. 'It's an open-source independent state, proper creative resistance' so anyone was welcome to play.

He showed me the flag of Sweetstopia. They spent months studying flags to come up with the design – a yellow triangle for Bohemianism, black for anarchy, red for the blood and sweat they put into renovating the homes, green for liberty and mother earth. Learning from the experience of Occupy at Parliament Square they experimented with communal consensus-based collective decision-making, and so far it was working well. There was a constant movement of residents, tending to the garden, gathering building materials to make repairs to the houses, returning with supplies from over the border. You could see this was a fully functioning autonomous community.

Daniel showed me inside the main house which had brightly painted cupboard doors and artwork daubed on the walls. What he called 'squatting technology' had been used to repair the water supply, essentially a garden hose that extended through a hole in the ceiling. The house had been restored with items recovered from the estate. 'This was the bohemian home', he announced as we made our way upstairs.

In one of the bedrooms the draft version of the founding credo of Sweetstopia was painted on the wall, 'We are Sweets Way and we are utopian bohemians'. It included ideas of creative resistance, sustainability, direct / participatory democracy. 'That led to a flag and having potato stamps for the passports', which Daniel picked up from the shelf, 'but we had to make new ones because the official stamps ended up in the compost'. He showed me a letter S carved into a gnarly spud 'from the utopian alphabet by Thomas More who invented Utopia'.

I ask Daniel what it meant to be a utopian bohemian. 'Well you've seen us in the 12 Bar being full on bohemian' and he explained how growing your own food in an urban environment was also part of it as a greener, cleaner, social experiment. 'We're trying to find a way to build our own Utopia'. He mentioned the community they set up in Friern Barnet library, which their occupation successfully saved, working together with local activists. What they were doing in Sweetstopia went beyond housing into broader principles to do with sustainability, democracy and creativity. The dog sleeping on the floor beside a mattress was the President of Sweetstopia. Daniel explained that Russell Brand narrowly missed out in the vote but he did send them some cakes, so he'd been offered the role of Minister of Propaganda.

It was a wonderful example of being the change you want to see in the world. 'A physical manifestation of these ideas', Daniel emphasised gesturing to the list on the wall. 'Love Rules without Rules' was their motto and it adorned the Sweetstopia passport which was only valid if you drew your own photo.

Back in the piazza garden beside a blue painted unicorn Steph listed the only rules of Sweetstopia: 'Please don't feed the unicorns and no knitting after dark'. Daniel added that they didn't have laws but had traditions instead as traditions can mutate and change as needed, although he emphasised that people had managed to adhere to the rule of not feeding the unicorns.

A pyramid of brightly coloured plastic, silver foil and wood had been constructed over a bathtub outside to make a spaceship for travel to other dimensions. All part of the 'play' aspect integral to the project. Vegas showed me her large papier-mâché mushroom inside the second house. The whole interior of the house was an artwork. The kitchen was wholesome and green. There was a pile of broccoli leaves picked to make a smoothie. There was also a free shop with clothes and books and toys you could take for free. It wasn't all artwork and inter-dimensional travel, there was a solidly practical aspect to the project as well. Steph continued the tour carrying a yoga mat. 'We skipped a jacuzzi, we don't have a working bath or shower in this house, we had to use the communal one.' A plumber who had just arrived on site was going to try and get the jacuzzi working in place of a bath.

The chill-out space was located in the lounge with large French windows looking out onto a garden. She created the space after they had to put the barricades up and it became a bit oppressive. She planned to get a big gong in the room to give everyone a sound bath. The house had also been used to run permaculture and meditation workshops for some of the local mums who stayed behind in the vacant houses with their kids. She'd painted 'Love You Are Not A Robot' on the wall in lurid patterns with psychedelic swirls, 'You Choose the Life You Create' painted on another.

Looking at the foliage dropping over the barricades around the garden, Steph told me how she worried that old maple and walnut trees on the estate would be cut down by the development. There will be a maple syrup harvest in March, and walnuts later in the year. They really could be fully self-sustaining here if free of the threat of eviction.

Steph tapped at a Tibetan singing bowl as we toured the house. The bedrooms were clean and tidy, clothes neatly stacked at the foot of made beds. There's a calm homely feel to the place, an atmosphere of 'goodness' that had somehow arisen from a site of conflict and destruction. There was magic here that cast an enchantment like the fairy realm of folklore: dwell too long and you might never leave. A small party escorted me to the border wall. I was given a send-off as a young woman, an 'anarchist fairy' stood in front of a pebble-dashed garage and played a wooden flute.

Sweetstopia lasted for another two months before being evicted by a posse of High Court bailiffs supported by seven vans of Metropolitan Police Officers. Along with the eviction of the Sweetstopians, the last surviving resident of Sweets Way was also hauled out of his home. Daniel, although arrested but not charged, was then unlawfully threatened with deportation from the UK, a charge he successfully contested. I would meet Daniel again later that year in a further act of creative resistance converting a disused old people's home in Golders Green into a social centre ahead of its proposed conversion into 'luxury apartments'. He then popped up in early 2018 when the utopian bohemians had established an Embassy of Conscience in Great Portland Street. The last I heard of Daniel he was up a tree somewhere along the River Colne protecting Mother Earth from the ravages of HS2. It's comforting to know there are people out there who won't rest until Utopia is built in the streets of London.

CHAPTER 6

AREAS OF OPPORTUNITY

Three months after the successful conclusion of the New Era campaign I found myself back in Hoxton for the opening of the Trew Era Café. Russell Brand had set up a social enterprise to provide training for people in abstinence-based recovery programmes in a vacant shop on the outside of the estate. Russell was delivered to the event by Chunky Mark the Artist Taxi Driver, a liaison it had given me great pleasure to set up.

The opening of the Trew Era became another mustering of the resistance, crammed into the tight space of the café and spilling out onto the pavement. The pressure was ratcheting up towards a general election, Russell still a focus of attention – so the opening of a café on an estate in the backstreets of Hoxton was being covered by multiple news crews. I caught up with some of the ladies from the New Era. Lynsay had brought along a delicious cake which was where I found Chunky Mark. Stacks of Russell's book Revolution sat beside jars of organic honey from Hackney, and packets of locally roasted coffee beans. Mark was enthused by the energy on display and the pushback against the forces attacking communities not just in London but across the country. 'It's great to see communities coming together, that's why it's special being here at the Trew Era Café', he declared as I thrust my camera towards his face.

There had been a momentum building up in the early part of 2015, and Mark was an important online voice. His Artist Taxi Driver persona produced a daily shot of energy through his single-take roadside rants on YouTube. He was keen to point out the role that Russell had played in providing an unlikely figure that people could rally around as he pointed to the huge crowd thronged outside on Pitfield Street. There was a strong positive energy radiating out from the Trew Era that day as Mark highlighted Russell's emphasis on 'caring' in his speech, a sentiment too frequently absent from the political discourse. 'There's a Kindness Bus out there, they're going "What's this all about?" It's because Russell's turned up.' He added that here was a man opening a café on a housing estate in East London who had just been named fourth in Prospect magazine's list of World Thinkers behind Yanis Varoufakis and Naomi Klein, and above Arundhati Roy and Daniel Kahneman. 'He's taking on Rupert Murdoch, he's taking on Fox News. Before Russell Brand came along we had Johnny Marbles,' the activist-comedian who threw a foam pie at Rupert Murdoch while he was giving evidence to a Parliamentary Committee.

2015 was a peculiar year, particularly the first six months. People were clamouring for Russell to put himself forward to stand for Mayor of London. He had briefly breached the office of the Mayor when appearing on BBC Question Time at City Hall and Boris Johnson had invited him in for tea. I'd been along in my role as researcher, briefing Russell on key points to raise with the Mayor in the show, such as the lack of genuinely affordable housing in the capital. I'd told Johnson that I'd just written a book about

London, 'So have I', he said and thrust a copy of The Greatest City on Earth – Ambitions for London into my hands with the words, 'Here you go, it's my last one', and off he went.

Among the briefing notes passed on to me by Boris's opponents in City Hall in preparation for Question Time, was the fact that Johnson was said to have held seven times more meetings with City bankers than with ordinary citizens of London and community groups. So you had to wonder what kind of ambitions he had for London as Mayor. Another note was that 77% of the election funds for his first Mayoral campaign were said to have come from the City, indicating where his true loyalties might lie. But maybe my cynicism, although informed by research, was misplaced.

'You don't have to be Aristotle to see that all policy and all debate and all public effort was aimed at the happiness and wellbeing of Londoners, and thereby of the people of the UK', it said in his booklet. Perhaps Boris deserved the benefit of the doubt even though during Question Time he had been caught out trumpeting the amount of affordable housing that was being created but having no idea what the definition of 'affordable' actually was – affordable for whom? The reality in 2015 was that you needed to earn £100,000 a year to be able to afford an 'affordable' home in Camden at a time when the average annual wage in London was £26,000.

The Book of Boris was a gospel of economic growth at all costs, a booming population, and skies filled with plane loads of overseas investors coming in to land at his new airport floating in the Thames estuary. It was an outburst of post-Olympian bravado, a boastful guffaw yelled from the apex of the Shard, pounding his chest, shouting at New Yorkers, Parisians and Berliners that 'mine is bigger than yours'. It was the crass yobbery of the Bullingdon Club draped in the chains of office putting Johnny Foreigner back in his place while selling him prize chunks of the family estate and

91

running off to Rio with the proceeds. And this was our Mayor – little did we know what was to come.

A map in the book highlighted 'Opportunity Areas', in some cases brownfield sites left vacant by post-industrial decline, while others were neighbourhoods with new transport links ripe for development. Some of these 'Opportunity Areas' were being snapped up by foreign investment funds and developers. Prime Minister David Cameron and Chinese President Xi Jinping celebrated a Beijing-based developer taking on a sizeable chunk of the Royal Docks, whilst the Qatari Royal Family had an interest in a lease on 51% of the former Olympic Village. With large amounts of property in Central London being acquired as 'buy to leave' investments that aimed to keep high-value sites empty, it was easy to see how the goal of greater inward investment may not have always had desirable outcomes. Indeed, the Guardian reported in July 2022 that with only a tenth of the Docklands development complete and none of the office space occupied, the Greater London Authority had 'kicked the developer off the project' and the future of the site was uncertain.

The map could be seen as a battleground where the future of London would be decided – Old Oak Common, Euston & King's Cross, Bishopsgate Goodsyard, Silicon Roundabout, Tottenham & the Upper Lea Valley, White City, Earls Court, the Lower Lea Valley and Stratford, Canada Water, Colindale, Wembley, Brent Cross – Cricklewood, Greenwich Peninsula, Woolwich, Barking Riverside to Dagenham Dock, Croydon, London Bridge and Borough, Elephant and Castle, Waterloo, Vauxhall-Nine Elms-Battersea. The list read like a tour of duty I was in the middle of. A wide blue strip of proposed development ran the length of London's Lea Valley and flowed out along the Thames to Dagenham. It seemed like an unstoppable wave of cascading towers.

Not far away from the Trew Era Café, where Hoxton crosses into Shoreditch, a cluster of community activists had formed a group to collectively oppose the sacking of the city. Reclaim London covered the walls of Red Gallery with 100 architectural elevations for proposed developments submitted to local planning authorities in London for an exhibition called Ubiquitous Unique. The architectural plans were stuck to the wall in neat rows to simply emphasise that despite claims of distinctiveness and references to the landscape they were all uniformly similar.

A sign on the wall of the Red Gallery was taken from a large estate agency bragging that with its chain of offices around the world it was best placed to reach the large worldwide market for London property. Their flier posted through the front doors of London homes declared that in 2014 '83% of London buyers came from overseas'.

Artist and Illustrator Lucinda Rogers was one of the people behind both the exhibition and the formation of Reclaim London. I'd met Lucinda back in 2002 when working with Russell Brand on a

TV pilot based on his madcap campaign to halt the redevelopment of Spitalfields Market. Lucy was involved in the actual, legitimate campaign – Spitalfields Market Under Threat or SMUT for short. She took our more theatrical interventions in good spirits and got back in touch some ten years later at the time of the publication of my book This Other London. When not fighting to save London's communities and built environment Lucy was a well-established artist, her illustrations appearing everywhere from national newspaper columns and the covers of Penguin paperbacks, to the collections of major museums and galleries. She saw herself as being from the tradition of 'the artist as reporter', in the spirit of the celebrated chronicler of off-beat London life, Geoffrey Fletcher.

Lucy talked me through the exhibition, how the big developments taking over London all looked the same, highlighting their uniformity by placing the principal elevations together in one space. Rows and rows of boxes of units. The exhibition created a startling collective image of a built environment becoming a bland vanilla architectural custard. Each plan claimed its own uniqueness despite all looking the same. They were not even uniquely unimaginative.

'You get the site, you draw a red line around it then you fill it with as many units as you can and then you start marketing them and making them sound very glamorous and tempting to buyers who are mostly coming from abroad. The needs for affordable housing are out of the picture', Lucy explained.

She pointed out some of the claims of developers that were borderline funny in their absurdity: the design for the massing of towers around the redevelopment of the Shell Centre on the South Bank was apparently inspired by the beautiful medieval architecture of San Geminagno in Tuscany. Some of the artists' impressions of completed schemes looked like the aftermath of an alien invasion – interstellar motherships landing on the Walworth Road.

It was a collage of dystopian silos of negative energy. These were plans for light-deprived communities pegged down by high rises that generated their own wind vortexes. Schemes that would not have passed a planning committee in communist East Germany were getting the go-ahead. The exhibition was a subtle thing that had an alarming impact.

Also looking around the exhibition, well acquainted with the coming horror, I spotted a couple of campaigners I'd first met earlier in the year when community activists mobilised to oppose the redevelopment of Earl's Court and Save Gibbs Green and West Kensington Estates, which had been earmarked for one of Boris Johnson's 'Opportunity Areas'.

Back on a cold, murky February morning, I'd turned up with my camera to meet with a colourful mustering of some of the most committed and resourceful community activists in the city. They stood outside one of the entrances to the building site that used to be the Earl's Court Exhibition Centre. The legendary venue that hosted Pink Floyd and the Ideal Home Show was reduced to a pile of rubble. It joined the ghost of the Empress Hall that preceded it, where Queen Victoria was said to visit, and where Buffalo Bill wowed London audiences with his Wild West Show. That too was demolished to be replaced by a block of flats.

There's a beguiling photo of Earl's Court Farm in the 1860s that popped up on my Facebook feed. The sepia print shows two wooden barns where a scattering of figures pose beside carts tipped forward. A large house stands in the background. There was the sense of open space, fields stretching through West Brompton to Eel Brook Common. The Counters Creek would still have been flowing through the fields from All Souls Cemetery in Kensal Green linking this great necropolis to another of the 'Magnificent Seven', Brompton Cemetery just over the road from Earl's Court. It's a peaceful rustic scene. We are haunted by these spectres of

London past. They have left their traces in the landscape, recorded memories in the buried rivers that gurgle beneath our feet.

We are haunted too by the visions of the London yet to come that the developers are committed to imposing upon us, wrenching people from their homes and raising ghost towers in their place. 'Vertical safe deposit boxes' with their own microclimates producing fierce winds to whip away pesky protestors like the dedicated cadre who'd gathered to ward off this macabre plot by the developers, Capco.

'I don't know what you've been told, Earl's Court has been sold. We are here to fight today, To keep privatisation far away' a woman in a Haz-Chem suit holding a placard reading 'Developers Keep Out' sang to the tune of the famous US Army cadence call. 'We're Still Here – Residents of Earls Court Say Evict Capco' read one of the handwritten banners. 'Stop Tearing the Heart out of London' was neatly printed and pinned on the end of a stick held aloft by a man in a beret and an overcoat adorned with badges. 'Save our 761 Homes', say the residents of West Kensington and Gibbs Green. Some of them are dressed in Haz-Chem suits to highlight the threat posed by the asbestos that could be released into the atmosphere by the demolition. The bright banner of the RMT railway workers union branch for the Piccadilly and District Line framed the scene as their Lillie Road Depot was also on the site and threatened with deletion. Transport for London was a stakeholder in the scheme.

I spoke to Aziz who had been in the hotel business in Earl's Court since the 1970s. He told me how 40-60% of his revenue came from the visitors to the Exhibition Centre – their profits per room had halved in that time – occupancy had fallen by around 75%. They'd been told the project would take 23 years to complete leaving local businesses such as his in limbo. He feared Earl's Court becoming a white elephant.

I also had a chat with Guy Rubin, Green Party candidate for Chelsea and Fulham whose interview was slightly undermined by the fluffy ears on the top of his grey woolly hat. He gave me a summary of what was happening. 'The Earl's Court Exhibition Centre will be demolished', local housing at West Kensington and Gibbs Green will also be demolished, '7,500 units of luxury housing will be built, there will also be tremendous environmental damage', and none of it was affordable, aimed solely at rich people, he says. 'I'm also concerned about the demolition of Earl's Court, an iconic local institution, which will have knock-on effects on local businesses', he told me. There were also questions about the valuation of the land which seemed to be too low for such a prime site resulting in calls for a public inquiry into the process.

A resident from West Ken and Gibbs Green recounted how the estate was somehow 'scooped' into the regeneration plot despite being outside the original boundary. At 77 acres it was the largest regeneration site outside China. 761 housing units on the estate were to be demolished, Local councillor Linda Wade stated, 'What we have here was a classic case of developer-led urban planning rather than urban planning responding to need'.

There was more singing. Despite the gravity of the situation spirits were high. This determined group could sense the righteousness of their cause. The protesters moved across the road from the site of the Exhibition Centre to the offices of the developers Capco. They had the best chants that I'd heard on any demonstration. I wonder if this contributed to the eventual success of their campaign against Capco.

'What shall we do with Boris Johnson, What shall we do with Boris Johnson Earl-eye in the morning, Kick him out and make him homeless', they sang replacing the Drunken Sailor with the then Mayor of London. A group in white Haz-Chem suits, some wearing face masks, formed a star-shaped die-in on the ground to illustrate the potential pollution risks. It was one of the best-staged protests I've covered.

'It's over a million for a studio flat in Earl's Court' said a lady as she stuck an eviction notice on the door of the Capco offices. 'We the People, Hereby serve notice on Capital & Counties Plc (Capco) on the Grounds of Social Cleansing, Economic and Cultural Vandalism. You are required forthwith to desist from further demolition, to re-instate what you have vandalised and to surrender your ownership of properties for the benefit of all.'

A year later I was back, this time for a historically themed protest to highlight the destruction of Empress Place and the Prince of Wales pub. This architecturally important mid-Victorian street was scheduled for demolition, boarded up and ready to be erased from the map. Another location to be added to London's long list of the disappeared. The homes stood as empty shells, echoes of former lives.

Protesters dressed as classic London characters serenaded by a solo violinist walked laps around Empress Place like a ritual to ward away the evil spirits of the speculative developers. Circling the ground, chanting, singing the music of the violinist, casting an enchantment of protection.

And it seemed to have worked. When I received an update from the campaign in the spring of 2020 the new Mayor of London, Sadiq Khan, had decided to take an interest in the site. The developers Capco eventually sold up in November 2019, apparently because the market for super prime homes collapsed in the Middle East and the Far East. The original development plans had been scrapped and the zone had shrunk to just over 25 acres. West Ken and Gibbs Green Estates were removed from the plans and had been saved, itself a major victory. Although the houses in Empress Place were still boarded up and empty, the Prince of Wales had been allowed to stay open and was serving beer and food when the 2020 lockdown restrictions were eased. Both exhibition centres have been demolished – the site was a wasteland.

Anabella told me that the campaign went on. The site had been bought by APG Group, a Dutch pension company with Delancey also holding a stake. The Delancey website read: 'Earl's Court Properties Limited (ECPL) was acquired in November 2019 by Delancey on behalf of its client fund and APG. It was a joint venture vehicle with Transport for London (TfL), and together we are bringing forward the redevelopment of the Earl's Court Opportunity Area.' Delancey was a name that took me back to the Olympic Park with their involvement in the former Athletes' Village in Stratford.

Technically speaking the land under the Exhibition Centre was public land, Anabella explained. The Campaign canvassed locals who wanted some kind of events venue on the site and they also wanted it to be 'Green'. They were campaigning for social housing and something that would provide employment for local people. Anabella told me the Grenfell disaster changed the way that the Kensington and Chelsea Council viewed social housing and made them take it more seriously.

The fact that we were having this conversation about the future of the Earl's Court site in 2020 was huge testament to the commitment and campaigning skill of that colourful band of protestors I'd met on a cold morning in February five years before. It was evidence that overwhelming odds could be defeated. A group of thirty or so local people had taken on a mighty megarich corporation who had the backing of the Mayor of London and they'd seen them both off. There was still power on the streets of London. Particularly if you had a good song or two.

CHAPTER 7

LEA VALLEY BURIAL MOUND PUNK

A May Day rooftop rendezvous with the Bermondsey Joyriders was to open unexpected new avenues. The irrepressible Henry Scott-Irvine from the Save Tin Pan Alley campaign had gained access to the roof of the old Foyles Building on Charing Cross Road and had organised a protest concert to highlight the threat to the area's musical and cultural heritage. Henry invited me along to witness and document the event.

I was met by Henry with a beaming smile outside Foyles and he told me how the tenants had been given 48 hours notice to vacate the building by the landlords, Soho Estates. Most of the tenants were artists and galleries who'd moved in after the bookshop relocated a few doors down Charing Cross Road to a swanky new store. However, the café had been run by the same people for 13 years and they'd sewn themselves into the fabric of the area.

The gig was being held not just to highlight the plight of those evicted from the Foyles Building but to raise awareness of what was happening around Soho and the bigger mission to Save London,

Henry told me. Some 'kick-ass rock and roll' blasted out over the rooftops as an act of solidarity and rebellion.

We made the long climb up the stairs of what was once one of London's most iconic shops. Having a dedicated window display there for my book This Other London was a real pinch-yourself moment. I used to come and look at the cover blown up to five feet high as people wandered past, not quite able to take it in.

From the rooftop, the skyline was dotted with cranes all around. Centre Point loomed over Charing Cross Road. Denmark Street lay dead opposite, the true epicentre of Henry's campaign. Soho Estates controlled a lot of the property in the area, Henry said as he railed into a microphone against the cynical corporate culture ripping the heart out of London. In the background, the Bermondsey Joyriders started warming up. It was like the Beatles on the rooftop of Apple Records in the 1960s.

As they were about to blast off, amps humming into the wind, Gary from the Joyriders talked about how he was concerned about what was happening in the area – the 12-Bar had been one of their favourite clubs, and the band were keen to help however they could. The Joyriders would produce a blues-punk-rock'n'roll howl of rage and disenchantment.

They launched into Right Now as people gazed up from Charing Cross Road and then slowly filtered up onto the rooftop. By the end of their third number Here Come the People Back Marching on the Street, a significant crowd had gathered for their rock and roll sermon about the state of London.

With the audience all around the rooftop, Henry made his appeal. 'Around you, you can see 16 cranes, these developers are the new enemy of society, the greedy, unaccountable property developer. These are the kind of people who are destroying homes.' He talked about fighting to make Denmark Street a music heritage zone, and as his speech wound down the Joyriders launched back into Here Come the People.

Post gig, chatting with lead singer and slide guitar wizard Gary
Lammin, all pearly punk king, he quietly dropped that they had
recently collaborated with counter-cultural legend John Sinclair
providing backing music for his London stand-up poetry gigs.
Sinclair had subsequently voiced the narration for their Noise and
Revolution album.

John Sinclair and his White Panther Party had formed a core
element of one of my many failed pitches to the BBC for a documentary about the equally failed revolutions of the 1960s. The
album, Gary told me, had been recorded in the depths of Epping
Forest dripping with punk resonances, within the orbit of Penny
Rimbaud and Gee Vaucher of Crass at their Dial House commune.
He offered to give me a copy of the album, a rock'n'roll statement
on the current state of London, and take me to some places of interest in the Forest. It was an offer too good to refuse.

I met Gary one morning a few days later at Loughton Station
to pick up a vinyl copy of the Noise and Revolution album, the
gatefold sleeve opening to reveal John Sinclair toking on a giant
Camberwell Carrot. He took me for a drive into Epping Forest, to
the studio where the great Sinclair had recorded his narration. I
had to conjure the image of this veteran of the Detroit garage rock
phenomenon making his way across the uneven rocky car park to
the row of old wooden farm buildings where the studio took up
residence next to a cat sanctuary where a clowder of captive felines
caterwauled incessantly. Here the man who launched Iggy Pop and
the MC5 upon the world, preparing the ground from which punk
would invade the culture, wrapped his pot-smoke-lacquered drawl
around Gary's words;

'At the outset the Bermondsey Joyriders were contemplating noise
and revolution / You see not only were the neighbourhoods being

torn apart by the greedy property developers but it was becoming obvious and very clear that things were disintegrating / Society was rapidly changing'.

This kicked off the album – a glam-punk-blues statement on the changing face of London in the claws of unchecked rapacious property development.

Gary talked me through the album as we slid round Forest roads to look at the esoteric zodiac reliefs on the ceiling of Waltham Abbey, dropping in nuggets of punk and rock'n'roll Forest lore – the pub where Hendrix played, the time in '75 when Malcolm Maclaren came to meet him at the Rodings Club at Manor Park all dandy-like, drinking G&Ts under the aggressive stares of after-work builders. Gary's band of the time, Cock Sparrer, were East London rockers in the spirit of East Ham's Small Faces, a cockney New York Dolls who put out a few singles on Decca Records. By 1979 he was rocking with Little Roosters and being played by John Peel on Radio 1.

Somewhere along the way between Waltham Abbey and Woodford I dropped in my interest in the prehistory of the area and aspects of its overlooked history. I mentioned a walk I'd done with my youngest son to explore the ancient earthworks of Ambresbury Banks and Loughton Camp. Gary said there was a person I'd have to meet, a man who'd be able to show me secrets of the Lea Valley region.

Two months later I was stood with Gary outside Pinehurst Community Centre and Eurofoods convenience store in the middle of a housing estate just outside Hertford. We'd been led here by the man Gary had mentioned, Dave Binns, a retired academic and longtime researcher into pre-Roman remains around London. That description doesn't do Dave's scope of knowledge proper justice – on the way up he gave me a recipe for a superfood stir-fry that included the magic ingredient of ground hemp seeds purchased from Asda.

We'd picked Dave up from his terraced house just off the North Circular. There seems to be some sort of connection between that pollution-spewing clotted artery and alternative visions of the outer reaches of London. My former walking buddy, Nick Papadimitriou, dreams of suburban mushroom gods and created a surreal narrative for the south Hertfordshire uplands from his tower block beside the North Circular at Golders Green. This road that loops within London never leaving, inspires escape from the City into the land of wooded hills just beyond. These dreamers take up a posting on the very edge of the urban fringe drawing sustenance from the metropolis and succour from the hinterland.

We attempted conversation sat in the back of Gary's Alfa – soft-top folded down, we were battered by turbulence hurtling out of London on the A10, the old Roman Ermine Street, but as Dave and I concurred, the supposed Roman roads were often laid along the routes of pre-existing trackways of greater antiquity. The Romans were just adept at improving and surfacing what would have been cruder thoroughfares.

The satnav wasn't so interested in uncovering the past and seemed intent on directing us into Hertford town centre which was bustling with Saturday lunchtime shoppers. Eventually, we traced the bus route that Dave had previously taken from Hertford station to Pinehurst estate. We parked up outside the shops and straight away saw that there beside the road was the mound – rising to around 5-6 feet above the ground. An old fella in tracksuit bottoms and slippers sloped away from the shop with two heavy bags of shopping as we took our first look.

Dave found the site in an archaeology book and stumbled around till he finally located the mound aided by a 1950s Ordnance Survey map. Stood there on the edge of the site, he announced that it was an Iron Age burial mound – almost certainly containing bodies, swords, and grave goods. Gary prompted him to recall the email from Hertford council (or it may have been Hertfordshire county council, he couldn't quite remember) confirming the authenticity of the site and linking to an archaeological report of a nearby location that referenced this particular barrow.

Despite being acknowledged by the council, Dave wasn't aware of any archaeological investigations into its contents. Could there really be bodies and grave goods still interred within the mound? Long barrows have been known to contain as many as 20-30 people. A long barrow on Therfield Heath, 20 miles north, also in Hertfordshire, was excavated in 1855 and 1935. Like this mound in Hertford, it sits on a high north-facing hill. Artefacts recovered spanned from the early Bronze Age to the early Iron Age, indicating that they could have been important places for the local population for centuries. Elsewhere in the country, Iron Age mounds have been found to contain chariots buried alongside the dead. Dave stated that elaborate burials would presumably have been reserved for high-status individuals with the agricultural revolution having produced new social hierarchies.

I hesitated when we first stepped onto the mound, wondering whether it was sacrilegious to walk over the slumbering dead from thousands of years before, but Dave strode forward and I followed his lead. He dated the site to 2500 years ago when they would have been taller with a steeper apex, comparable to the famous earthwork at Avebury. In some cases, he speculated, the mounds may have risen to a point like earth pyramids. He went into a gentle-voiced reverie: 'It's the sweep of the curve of the ancient barrows that gives them their magic'.

Dave tentatively proposed that given the position of the mounds, rising above the River Lea which slides past at the bottom of a steep cliff, and occupying a dominant position looking out across the Lea

Valley, they were perhaps displays of political power by elite families in the region, 'exercising a certain authority and power over the domain which they preside over, and a symbolic statement of that emergent elite'.

That elite and their power, Dave expanded, emerged from the Neolithic 'revolution' that came out of the domestication of animals which allowed for a surplus of food to be produced and a division of labour. 'What we are seeing with structures like this, is a kind of crystallisation in the landscape, a physical crystallisation which is an expression of behaviour: people transforming the landscape'.

This was music to Gary's fuzz guitar ears: 'That is spot on man'.

'We have class society and the State because you have dominant groups and individuals apparently regulating this process of construction,' Dave continued, but doubting this was an entirely coercive process, and wondering what made people dispense with their hunter-gatherer existence to lug tons of soil into giant earth structures?

Dave turned to look across the mound with its necklace of brown brick semis:

'What we are talking about, this is what is beautiful, is the still visible crystallisation of the social, cultural and political emergence of class society and the state – all of our problems'.

Suddenly the mound lost any vestiges of its arcadian past, and appeared before me as a Neolithic Westfield.

A tarmac path ran around the edge of the mound, cars pootled past, and people ambled by on their way home. The location had none of the trappings and adornments of the celebrated sites of similar antiquity, there wasn't even a small plaque to acknowledge its heritage. Somehow that gave it more power, that it sat there lurking amongst the familiar suburban mundanity, witnessing waves of change over thousands of years. A silent sentinel still watching over the domain of the original mound builders. There were no solstice pilgrims congregating on the Pinehurst estate, no gift shop, just the markings on the OS map.

We worked our way through the elaborate maze of houses to descend to the valley floor. A mock stone circle had been laid out as a commissioned piece of public art, perhaps as a nod towards the tumulus nearby. On the edge of the estate, there were views over rooftops across the Lea Valley to Cowshed Corner and a sense of how the mound would have dominated a significant position in the upper Lea Valley close to a bend in the river. On the far side of that bend, the Iron Age Widbury hillfort stood guard over the valley. Just beyond the fort is a tumulus in Easneye Wood overlooking the River Ash, a tributary of the Lea. Also, later earthworks were built beside the river at Hertford to defend the area against the invading Danes.

Dave later expanded that by looking back into the origins of our current divisions, it would be possible to envision their overthrow. This mound of earth and bones in the middle of a housing estate in the upper Lea Valley was a symbol of the beginnings of the struggles I'd been witnessing across London – the claiming of the land by dominant groups, hierarchies marked in the landscape.

We picked up a set of steps leading down beneath where the A10 passed overhead on a giant concrete viaduct and the river snaked through King's Meads. As the traffic rattled past obliterating the audio on my pocket camera, Dave talked of how Ware was said to be one of the oldest continually occupied sites in Europe. He believed that the consistent pattern of prehistoric development along the Lea indicated its cultural importance – including 'magnificent Neolithic earthworks', Waulud's Bank, at the source of the river in Luton. These structures were created in relation to the Lea, he said. I asked if the Lea is our Ganges, a sacred river? He hesitated to

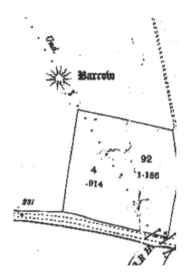

Above: The Barrow as shown on the 1898 Ordnance Survey map
Below: Tumulus marked on the 1938 OS map

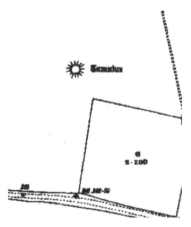

Source: An Archaeological Evaluation for Bride Hall Development Limited
by Sarah Coles, Thames Valley Archaeological Services, January 2000

give it that status: 'There may not have been the cultural distinction between the sacred and the secular' as there is in our current culture. The Thames has produced an impressive array of artefacts possibly dispensed into the waters as votive offerings – what treasures lie in the silt bed of the Lea awaiting discovery?

Looking back along the concrete path from this vantage point I half-joked that it could be following the traces of a route that dates from the building of the mound around 2500 years ago. The 1898 OS map does show the dotted line of a footpath across the fields so that idea is not as fanciful as it first appeared. The juxtaposition of uninspired 1970s paving and the idea of Neolithic trackways with notions of ley lines tickled me as a conceit, although it could be grounded in some kind of pragmatic fact that this was the best pass to the top of the Pinehurst ridge.

Dave raised the question of the pre-Roman origins of Ermine Street which runs next to the mound. 'This is where Ermine Street crosses the Lea' he pointed out. It would therefore have been an important location, the site of a bridge or a ford, 'a venerable ancient way crossing an important river' adding to the wider context of the site and the pattern of long-term occupation in the area.

Gary the punk-bluesman tunes into the theme of crossroads as a reference point springing from the Robert Johnson song of 1936 set at the intersection of Highways 61 and 49 in rural Mississippi, and fuelling the myth of Johnson trading his soul with the Devil in return for the gift of music. Gary acquired his slide guitar prowess on the Isle of Dogs, that alluvial tongue supping on the long meander of the Thames – another site associated with great symbolic power and now colonised by the towers of Mammon at Canary Wharf.

As we climbed the steps, tongue in cheek Dave said that by

building the steps as they had – along wide brick pillars broken up into a series of stages – unwittingly the builders had created the sense of a processional way, the kind of avenues laid out over miles in prehistory leading up to stone circles and sacred sites. 'It's as if we're being guided' he said with a smile. Whether that was down to the bus stop or up to Eurofoods doesn't much matter – we know we're bound for the burial mound.

We did a final pass over and around the mound. Such a modest location seemed to radiate meaning that we couldn't quite grasp at that juncture. This was more than a day trip up the Lea Valley to the fringe of London. It was linked to the Foyles rooftop on Charing Cross Road and Henry Scott-Irvine railing against the developers destroying London's heritage. Through Gary and Dave and punk blues guitar but also via a deeper thread.

At home that night I re-examined my OS map of the Lea Valley, where the Pinehurst Mound sneaks in the top corner. I was excited to spot another tumulus marked on the OS map on the opposite flank of the Lea Valley from Pinehurst, in Easneye Wood. Were these sites connected to the Bronze Age settlements also by the Lea further down the river in the Olympic Park at Stratford and at Leyton?

An archaeological report from January 2000 conducted when a drive-through McDonald's and more housing were built adjacent to Pinehurst noted that the housing estate was built on a golf course where the barrow had stood in open space. The 'upstanding bowl barrow' dated from the early Bronze Age and as of the year 2000 had not been excavated. A number of other Bronze Age sites had been recorded in the immediate area including a 'ring-ditch enclosure probably dating to the Neolithic or Bronze Age' with a settlement located to the northeast. We were standing in the centre of a major Bronze Age development.

A report from the London and Middlesex Archaeological Society detailed excavations in Edmonton around Plevna and Montagu Roads, on the Lea floodplain south of Pinehurst, that suggested human habitation in the area right through from the Mesolithic era with indicators of a significant Bronze Age settlement. There were multiple other sites of a similar age throughout the Lea Valley region and over the high ground into Epping Forest.

The proliferation of prehistoric sites nearer the source of Lea threw up the interesting possibility that the upper Lea Valley was the source of the city – that London had been a prehistoric satellite of a great civilisation spreading across the high lands of Hertfordshire. It had been posited by H Ormsby in his 1924 book London on the Thames that a major pre-Roman British line of communication ran along the western edge of the Lea Valley that possibly linked a port near the confluence with the Thames with Ware and Hertford then onwards to the upper Colne and Verulam. This was part of a communication route that connected with the continent before the Romans built their port further along the Thames shifting the city's centre of power westwards.

It was a tantalising question that warranted further investigation. With Dave's words ringing in my ears that by studying mounds we could see the very emergence of class society and the origins of all our contemporary problems, I knew this was a quest that would have to continue beyond the sleepy estate on the outskirts between Ware and Hertford.

CHAPTER 8

THE ROAD TO EASNEYE – LEYTONSTONE TO RYE HOUSE

The white envelope the Postie held out to me as I stood at the front door in my pants clutching the pug under my arm, was manically sealed with about half a roll of brown packing tape. Slicing my way inside felt like an act of archaeology itself, careful not to damage the delicate ancient artefact inside – a two-page pamphlet bound in an orange card cover for which I'd paid £1.99 from a book dealer in Peterborough. A sticker on the cover bore the title, Opening of a Barrow in Easneye Wood, Hertfordshire. Evans, J. Transactions of the East Hertfordshire Archaeological Society, Volume 1, Part 2, 1900.

The first of the two pages was a black and white photograph of an old lady in a heavy black Victorian coat and hat stood around half-way up the burial mound. Behind her sat a boy near the summit gazing straight down the lens of the camera. The tree foliage around the barrow appeared smudged giving the photo a painterly touch. I felt a tingling sensation at this glimpse back through time holding the photo of a location that was itself a portal to a far more distant past. But also, as it marked the first (and last?) time the tumulus had been opened in over 2000 years.

In the pamphlet, Sir John Evans described witnessing Mr T Fowell Buxton, the owner of Easneye Wood, excavating the barrow with his son Mr John Henry Buxton on 19th July 1899. As a local antiquarian, Evans had been called upon to 'undertake the superintendence' of the dig.

The barrow, then as now, sits in Easneye Wood, and at that point in time was not marked on the Ordnance Survey map. The mound is 60 feet in diameter and 10 feet tall and it's interesting how Evans hoped it was of Roman origin rather than of an earlier date. He noted the nearby Youngsbury Roman burial mound three miles away, which had been excavated in 1889. 'These hopes were doomed to be disappointed', he stated. 'A trench about three feet wide was cut in the barrow from the south to the centre, and was carried down to about two feet below the original surface of the ground. As the centre was approached traces of burning became evident... and eventually beneath a slab of partially charred wood a considerable deposit of burnt bones was discovered.'

His disappointment was evident as he wrote, 'Not a solitary piece of pottery, not a fragment of bronze, nor a single worked flint was found, such as might possibly have assisted in determining the date at which these burnt bones were deposited'. The only nonhuman artefact was the 'jaw-bone of a young pig'. Due to the presence of the bones alone, he concluded that the mound was of pre-Roman origin, characteristic of 'many others'. Evans sounded bored and thwarted.

This reaction perplexed me – whereas I had abandoned plans for a walk to Youngsbury Mound on the basis that it was merely another Roman site, Evans and Buxton had seemingly opened the tumulus in the hope of discovering Roman remains. Was this merely a case of treasure hunting or was it indicative of a Victorian admiration of the classical world over their perception of our barbarian prehistoric past?

The charred remains of the body were sent to 'the well-known anatomist' JG Garson who could only report that the bones belonged to an adult of indeterminate age or gender. 'The bones and ashes were, after examination, placed in an earthenware jar, with an inscription on a copper plate stating when and by whom the barrow was opened, and what was found in it. The jar, with its contents, was placed in the centre of the mound, where the bones were discovered, and the earth was replaced in the excavation.' And where they presumably still lie.

Who was the person cremated and then buried alone with a young pig? A prehistoric proto-Londoner looking down the Lea Valley from the crest of Easneye Wood.

I was so fixated on the report of the excavation that I at first missed the significance of the name of the two men who'd opened the mound. A quick Google search revealed that they were prominent members of the famous Buxton family. Furthermore, Thomas Fowell Buxton had lived at Leytonstone House before moving to Easneye.

The Buxtons were an incredibly influential family, but their habit of continuously re-using the same names and marrying members of the same family made untangling their illustrious history a complicated affair. The Thomas Fowell Buxton who was father to the Thomas Fowell Buxton who lived at Leytonstone House and excavated the Easneye mound, was an MP and noted social reformer who campaigned for the abolition of slavery. His mother was Anna Hanbury, whose family co-owned the Truman, Hanbury and Co brewery in Brick Lane. After Thomas was made a partner the brewery became Truman, Hanbury and Buxton.

Luckily there's a varnished board displaying information about the Buxtons of Leytonstone House next to the cashpoints at Tesco in Leytonstone. It simplified the narrative to that of Sir Edward North Buxton – son of Thomas Fowell the abolitionist – and mentioned the connection through marriage with the Gurney family of Quaker bankers who were involved in the merger that formed the modern Barclays Bank. It pointed out how the Buxtons of Leytonstone were active in 'fighting the cause of the commoners in Epping Forest' which led to the Epping Forest Act of 1878 preserving the Forest at a time of encroachment by builders. Edward North Buxton became a verderer of Epping Forest and his classic Epping Forest guidebook from 1888 accompanies me on all my forays into the forest. A grainy photo of him stares out across the scattered trollies. There was now a direct link between the upper Lea Valley burial mounds and my home territory in Leytonstone. And also, to a family whose history is entwined with the development of Victorian London.

The Buxton revelation made my fascination with the Pinehurst Mound suddenly make sense. I'll be honest, when I realised where we were that day with Gary and Dave my heart sank a little, it was too far outside the zone of my research and probably wouldn't tell me anything in my search for understanding of the changing face of London. But the experience wouldn't leave me and followed me all summer. I kept revisiting the video I shot that day and scanning various OS maps, circling tumuli and hillforts in the Lea Valley area. I read and reread the archaeological reports of sites around the region. I was taking it seriously enough to do this work at home rather than in the last hour's drinking in the pub with papers and maps spread out over a table.

I'd been making excursions in recent years from Leytonstone through the Forest and along the Lea, often winding up at Chingford, Ponders End, Broxbourne – good places to take in the

116

glorious Lea Valley sunsets. I could sense something starting to co-here but the image was still fuzzy and out of focus. The only thing to do was to walk the ground and see what emerged. A ritualistic perambulation to exorcise whatever had been unleashed up on the Pinehurst Mound.

It wasn't so easy to carve out time for a day-long schlep now that I was a full-time stay-at-home Dad, but I must have bothered my wife so much with ramblings about networks of prehistoric sites that in the end I was virtually ordered from the house to get it out of my system. One September Sunday I set off at 1pm, walking away from Leytonstone's Car Free Day and Big Weekender. A bass drum throbbed from the stage erected at the bus station. The Selector would find themselves sound-checking facing a row of empty bus shelters – the 66 to Romford, the 145 to Dagenham Asda. At least one member of the band must've reflected on former glories and wondered how it had come to this: 'Once we sold out Newcastle City Hall and now we're playing a bus station in Leytonstone'.

The stalls lining Church Lane were a concoction – African carvings, brightly woven baskets, batik print fabrics – an ersatz hippydom, a poor re-enactment of 1960s Haight Ashbury. It's a car driver's idea of what a car free day would look like. Somebody did a performance of bubble blowing and nearly got splattered by the 257 bus to Walthamstow.

The early car free crowds thinned out as the High Road climbed towards the forest. The Wetherspoons had a smattering of lunchtime drinkers and pub grub munchers. It's easy to overlook the names of Wetherspoons pubs – so powerful is the collective branding – but the names often carry local significance. This one is called the Walnut Tree and it was only when flicking through WG Hammock's 1904 Leytonstone and its History in said pub that I came across a reference to Walnut Tree Cottage resided in by William Whittingham who owned land further along the High Road.

Facing the Wetherspoons across Gainsborough Road is a drive-thru McDonalds where I've had cause to ponder on the state of my life stood there in a queue for a Quarter Pounder with Cheese at 1.30am after being ejected from the Walnut Tree. This appears to have been the site of Gainsborough House, occupied at the time of Hammock's writing in 1904 by a Dr Jekyll. It cannot have been easy to carry the name Dr Jekyll after the success of Robert Louis Stevenson's book Dr Jekyll and Mr Hyde even though the literary Jekyll was a Reverend from Godalming and a friend of Stevenson's. The Leytonstone Dr Jekyll died in 1933 and was buried in Wanstead, his sons Joseph and Nugent also became doctors, were baptised in the local parish church and lived in Gainsborough House.

Tesco's car park covers the high ground on Gainsborough Road, once a field belonging to the farmer, Mr Payze, where a footpath cut across open land to Leyton. Where people lugged their weekly shops today was once a bucolic scene, 'straw-littered, with its large black gate and black thatched barn, and then, beyond, a number of cottages with gardens which were always bright with flowers'. Car Free Day has come a bit late.

Mr Payze was also the landlord of the Crown pub across the other side of the High Road which still stands. I was drawn there when I first moved to the area by the legendary What's Cookin' 'rockin country fried' music nights. Earlier that summer I saw guitarist John Ellis perform a solo set in the upstairs room to an audience of about 12 people. John, a Leytonstoner, was a founder member of seminal punk band The Vibrators – later playing with The Stranglers (he also toured with Peter Gabriel). In between songs John recounted anecdotes and before launching into a sequence of acoustic punk tunes talked about how in the early 1970s he'd been influenced by reading John Michell's The View Over Atlantis. This had been one of the books that popularized the notion of ley lines connecting megalithic monuments and powerful points in the landscape. Around the same time, punk became a populist vehicle for the philosophies of Guy Debord and the Situationist International, a bunch of louche Left-Bank intellectuals who'd nearly overthrown the French government in 1968, but more importantly for me, codified the practice of wandering around the unpromising quarters of cities and writing about it in an obscure and oblique manner. By daubing urban rambling with the pseudo-scientific label of psychogeography the practice gained a certain cachet. In London, it got hybridized with Michell's earth mysteries and punk rock to form a more potent brew – not just 'walking with attitude' but with a healthy dose of mysticism and Druidry. Guy Debord in his corduroy jacket and roll neck puffing a Gaullois looked a bit square – Johnny Rotten and Sid Vicious were cool and terrifying, the art-school educated svengali Malcolm Maclaren passing notes in the background. Psychogeography was later further embedded in punk lore by featuring in Greil Marcus's definitive book on the genre, Lipstick Traces, and now those smeared red lines seemed to lead back to this high ground in Leytonstone.

Hearing John knock out acoustic versions of Vibrators and Stranglers tunes above the Crown and talking about ley lines threw up another connection in the Punk-Epping Forest Nexus – Gary Lammin in Loughton, Penny Rimbaud of Crass at the Dial House in Ongar, and now John Ellis in Leytonstone. This should be plotted out on a map rather than alignments between the standing stones at Avebury.

Maybe the link was also there in my namesake John Rogers the Martyr who sought refuge in the Forest after being accused of heresy. Greil Marcus links punk to medieval English heretics. Rogers' crime was to translate the Latin bible into English – so that the supposed word of God was written in the word of the street. People would no longer need to listen to sermons in an incomprehensible dead foreign language, they could hear the deity speak in their own tongue without a priest to act as interpreter. A dangerous idea that had to be brutally suppressed.

The smashing of old orders was also what punk was supposed to be about – gobbing a throat full of phlegm on the notion that you needed to be a trained musician to form a band and get on stage. Anyone could play guitar, anyone could write a song, and you didn't need a pop priest to tell you what music sounded like. I'm proud to share a name with John Rogers the Heretic even though I couldn't have refused my children begging me to recant my heresy to save my life as the other JR did. Let's hope a kinder fate awaits these three-chord heroes than dear old John Rogers, taken from the Forest on the back of a cart, possibly down the road outside the Crown, and burnt at the stake in Smithfield in 1555.

This trek to the Easneye mound had been designed to start at Leytonstone House – home of the Buxtons and to me now a significant nodal point in the Lea Valley. It was possible that they'd made the journey I was embarking on from Leytonstone to Easneye near Ware. Where I travelled on foot and bus, I guess they would have clattered over rough forest roads by horse-drawn carriage. Today Leytonstone House is the office of a firm of chartered accountants. After the Buxtons moved on, Leytonstone House became a home for the 'juvenile poor' run by the Bethnal Green Board of Guardians.

Standing in the car park in front of Leytonstone House I imagined EN Buxton looking out of one of the upstairs windows across the Green Man roundabout planning his walks into the Forest that I now follow. His heart would sink at the traffic carnage of the M11

Link Road, but the forest paths he mapped are still there once you escape the road.

Passages led under the Green Man roundabout. It's said that Dick Turpin had a tunnel here that led from the Green Man pub into the Forest. There's barely a drinking house of the correct age around the fringe of London that doesn't claim a connection to the notorious highwayman. But given that Dick was a native of the area, the Green Man had a greater claim than most. It's also believed that he had a cave at High Beach. Hammock writes that in 1698 cavalry patrolled the roads that marked the border between Essex and Middlesex due to the threat from bandits, and that 'mounted and masked highwaymen' stalking Leyton Heath were mentioned in letters from 1597. Church registers record an inquest into the shooting of a highwayman in 1746.

There's been a pub on the site of the Green Man since at least 1670. Vestry meetings were recorded here in 1703 where it was decided which parish was responsible for repairs to the bridge across the road to Stratford at Holloway Down (the costs fell to the parish of Wanstead somehow). It was the staging post for many a sojourn in the forest glades. Rudolph Rocker recounted drinking here at the start of anarchist day trips he organised from Whitechapel at the end of the 19th century. Film-maker Adam Kossoff (of the famous East End family of bakers and artists) lives near the Green Man and made a film about Rocker which I screened that summer in the children's centre at Harrow Green, not far from the bridge that the burghers of Wanstead had to repair.

These final summer days are the most precious of the year, the last hurrah of late sunsets. Soon the tall dry grasses receded and the ground became a swamp. Many times, I've followed the route in EN Buxton's book from Leytonstone to Woodford then on to Chingford. The beautiful colour map by Stanfords in my 1923 edition, 9th reprint, of Epping Forest shows this first section as Leyton Flats. Buxton describes it as 'a level open space, much broken by old gravel pits, and covered with patches of gorse and broom. It's almost free from trees, and the few that are left have been seriously stunted and injured by the reckless gravel-digging of former years.' The gorse and broom remained but the trees seem to have recovered from their traumas – there are some mighty oaks old enough to have seen Buxton striding along the footpaths which may also have witnessed the last days of the highwaymen.

It was a normal Sunday scene over by the Hollow Ponds – dogs, joggers, picnics, families, canoodling couples, the ever-hungry geese. A sausage dog passed proudly carrying a blue ball the size of its head. A decomposing body was found in the trees by the Hollow Ponds by a passing member of the public who noticed a frenzied swarm of rats around a blue Ikea bag, just four days before my walk.

The body was identified as belonging to a 53-year-old Turkish man called Hidir Aksakal, also known as Boxer Cetin who'd been murdered sometime before elsewhere. Our quiet corner of Leytonstone was all over the news for the first time since the intense wildfires of two summers previously.

As I walked from the Tea Hut through the carpark crunching fallen cob nuts underfoot, I wondered if I was following the killer's steps. Families played and ate ice cream right next to police vans. It was peculiar to see people licking Mr Whippy beside red and white incident tape where a body had sat rotting in a shopping bag. Forensics officers in blue plastic overalls moved in and out of the trees near the boating shed. Bobbies sipped tea stood by the open doors of their cars. People rowed boats on the Hollow Ponds.

I ducked into the trees on the other side of Whipps Cross Road and realised that I was urinating onto the edge of a blue tarpaulin shelter, somebody's home in the roadside undergrowth. These makeshift dwellings can be spotted on the edges of open spaces around the fringes of London. Sometimes great care is taken to hang clothes and arrange possessions. The old tramp colonies reported by depression-era topographers were returning.

Things happen in the trees around the Ponds. A thread on the local Facebook page erupted when somebody stumbled upon two men kissing and it had to be pointed out that this was a historic gay cruising spot with an important part in the story of Gay London. In 2008 a fisherman heard rustling in the trees and saw a four-foot tall 'hairy, dark creature' in the undergrowth. People still go looking for the Hollow Ponds Bear although there haven't been any further sightings that I'm aware of. On summer evenings pipistrelle bats carve patterns in the fly-thick air. The trees on the far side from Whipps Cross Road hide the dried-up footprint of Leytonstone Lido, now littered with condom wrappers and discarded wet wipes.

The Hollow Ponds had only just been mythologised in song by Leytonstone-born ex-Blur frontman Damon Albarn, who was subsequently honoured with a Blue Plaque on the house where he grew up in Fillebrook Road. The languid lament of childhood memories recalled the heatwave of 1976, the destruction of the majority of Fillebrook Road by the M11 Link Road, freely roaming horses and the Green Man. It's a dreamy downbeat tune. I went round the corner on the day the plaque was unveiled: low-key like the song, a handful of us stood in the street on a chilly October morning, Albarn arrived with his family, bleary-eyed and cheerful, warmly hugging the present occupants of the house before posing for photos leaning from his old bedroom window. The photos and video I shot were viewed by Blur fans around the world – particularly in Japan and Brazil. Hopefully, the song will work its way back up the Google rankings to replace the grisly death of Boxer Cetin in the popular consciousness.

I crossed Lea Bridge roundabout, which has always felt like the edge of London to me with the rest of the city to the west tethered like a ball on a string. There were road signs that warned of crossing cattle. The glades of Epping Forest define the journey beyond into Essex. I moved on to Shernhall Street to get the bus north to Sewardstone. This is one of the older thoroughfares in the area after you have taken into consideration the Roman roads leading from the city to Colchester. Was it part of the pilgrimage route to Waltham Abbey? Leyton High Road formed one section of the path from Stratford Abbey to the Holy Cross but was there a route from Barking Abbey further east that stuck to the high ground? It may also have been the ancient way linking Bronze and Iron Age settlements of the upper Lea Valley to the tribal camps in the forest.

My pilgrimage would stretch beyond Waltham Abbey and I'd be progressing not on a mule, or even on foot at this point, but on a W16 bus to Chingford Mount. I was serenaded in my mind by Gus

Elen's 1899 music hall hit, If it Wasn't for the 'Ouses in Between reciting distant rural views from his cramped city garden, taking in Chingford and Rye House 'from the cock-loft could be seen'. The bus glided past The Viking Store on Wood Street, Walthamstow perhaps drawn here by the oscillating Nordic heritage permeating through the gravels from the Viking incursions up the River Lea which then became the border between the Dane Law and English Law. Or perhaps the rent was reasonable.

The W16 had taken us on one of our first family outings when we moved to Leytonstone and looked to explore the hinterland. All I knew about Chingford Mount at that time was that it was mentioned in Iain Sinclair's Lights Out for the Territory. It was in the record-breaking summer of 2006 that made Damon Albarn's summer of 1976 seem balmy by comparison. Hyde Park turned into a burnt grassless desert, something that has since become the summer norm. After walking through the cemetery we found our way into Ridgeway Park occupying an elevated spur overlooking the Lea Valley reservoirs and the tower blocks at Ponders End. The boys rode on the miniature railway clutching a bag of pink candy-floss and we ate a picnic in the shade of an enormous bush hiding from the punishing sun. I've been drawn out this way on foot ever since. Forest walks from Leytonstone necessarily pass through the bottle-neck at Highams Park, where the River Ching meanders along a deep-sided smooth brown channel, exposed tree roots cro-cheted into the earth, a network of wooden bridges criss-crossing the stream. It feels mythical.

Chingford has never fully accepted being absorbed into London in 1965 when it left the county of Essex and became part of the newly formed London borough of Waltham Forest. Letters from Chingford residents to the Waltham Forest Guardian were still sometimes signed from 'Chingford, Essex'.

The previous midsummer I emerged parched and hungry from the Forest after walking from Woodford without water and ventured along the High Street for the first time. Sams Quality Fish and Chip Restaurant on Chingford Green shimmered like an oasis, the jaundice yellow strip lights drew me in. I ate battered sausage and chips on a bench near the church watching dignified old folk with rows of military medals pinned to their blazers filing into the Assembly Hall guarded by boys in uniform for a performance by the Ex-Servicemen's Wives Choir. It was like the 1950s. A place that seemed so incongruous in modern London, like one of those 'out-of-place artefacts' that defy the conventional understanding of human history.

That day too I was bound for Sewardstone with a desire to hit this obscure outer corner of London, the true city limits. After finishing the sausage and chips, a path at the rear of the Kings Head pub led me to the summit of Pole Hill where a stone obelisk bears two plaques. The first records the association with TE Lawrence (of Arabia – forever in my mind Peter O'Toole garbed in white and directed by David Lean) who bought 18 acres on Pole Hill. He planned to build a house here with his friend Vyvyan Richards and print his now-famous work The Seven Pillars of Wisdom. The dream remained unfulfilled, but they did build a hut with a pool where Richards lived until 1922.

The second plaque reads: 'This pillar was erected in 1824 under the direction of the Reverend John Pound MA Astronomer Royal. It was placed on the Greenwich Meridian and its purpose was to indicate the direction of true north from the transit telescope of the Royal Observatory. The Greenwich Meridian was changed in 1850 and adopted by international agreement in 1884 as the line of zero longitude, passing 19 feet to the east of this pillar.'

Chingford Green wasn't the land that time forgot, but the place where time began. It wasn't the 1950s down there – it was the year 130.

I passed on through Hawk Wood and ascended Yardley Hill through a field of buttercups and was rewarded with incredible views down the Lea Valley and across to the Northern Heights. The last of the evening summer sun broke through the cloud cover as another expansive view opened up from the edge of Fernhill Wood, a heavenly luminosity spilling down blessing Brimsdown Power Station. That walk had ended with a steep descent down a long farm track to Sewardstone from Barn Hill as the daylight faded after 9pm, before schlepping in the twilight towards Waltham Abbey and a train back into London from Waltham Cross.

Today I would need to truncate that section of the journey – arriving at London's city limits on a 'summer season only' bus to the Lea Valley Campsite. I was the solitary passenger to ride the 215 to its terminus at the point where London gives way to Essex. Sewardstone threw up the curious anomaly of being the only place outside Greater London with a London postcode, E4. A bit of trivia for your next pub quiz.

The idea of passing out of London was only notional in this case – the gravitational centre here is not the City or Westminster but the Lea Valley. In London's Forest published in 1909 Percival JS Perceval (now that's a name) offered up this tantalising idea about the original meaning of both the name and geology of the area. 'Sewardstone, below High Beach, twelve miles from London, is considered by some to have been anciently the Seward-stone, indicating the spot where the tide from the sea turned.' He based this fanciful notion on the fact that Essex was the most recent region to have risen from the sea after the Eocene period. He pointed out that the marshy soil had given up a wealth of fossils – mammoths, great ox, giant deer, elk, lions, and bears. The more realistic origin was that it was named after a Saxon called 'Syward' or 'Seward' as indeed Perceval acknowledged.

It was 3 pm and the real walk was only just beginning. Sunset was around 7.15 and there was a significant trek ahead. I loaded up on veg samosas in the Esso garage to fuel the journey. Brimsdown Power Station shimmered across the Lea. Most Londoners had no connection to where their power originated, up here poking out of the marsh mud, a two hour walk from New Hackney. As I contemplated the task at hand and ran a system check on my body, I deduced that I didn't feel good in myself, heavy-legged and lethargic. If I were a plane on the runway I'd be grounded for maintenance. How on earth would I make it 11.5 miles to Easneye Wood and locate the burial mound?

I passed Netherhouse Farm on the long stretch of road into Waltham Abbey. Did the pilgrims weary at this point, the bones of their old asses groaning under the sagging guts of the riders? The pilgrim route out of London didn't end at Waltham Abbey but continued to Walsingham, the main attraction. The wayside was marked with churches, chapels and hospices that offered refreshment. The Premier Inn advertised 'Fizz Friday' keeping the tradition alive. This was the point of release as you walked out of London, a strange trepidation creeping up the spine, uplands stretching out ahead. Beyond lay England.

Leytonstone – Chingford – Waltham Abbey may not be the pilgrim route but it is the David Beckham trail – promoted more enthusiastically by the local authority than any ecclesiastical heritage. Born in Whipps Cross Hospital by the Hollow Ponds, his family followed the path of many on the up before them, gradually nudging out into Essex with the City still in view on a clear day – the reversal of Gus Elen's tune, the ancestral stomping grounds in sight.

The M25 pulsed under the bridge. Where are they all going, I always wonder, and in such a hurry. Barneys Seafood stall in the carpark of Barneys Pub confirmed that I was on the Beckham trail. There was a seafood stall outside Chingford United Services Club.

I wonder if cockle stalls have popped up in Madrid, Paris, Milan and Los Angeles too, wherever Becks has plied his trade.

A municipal sign welcoming the traveller to Waltham Abbey pointed out an arguably more significant association – that the Abbey is the final resting place of King Harold II – the last Saxon King of England. Although it is not the presence of Harold's body that made Waltham a place of pilgrimage, that had been established shortly before his death at the Battle of Hastings.

On my visit to the Abbey with Gary Lammin I'd picked up a pamphlet in the crypt shop telling the Legend of the Miraculous Cross of Waltham translated from a text written down by a Canon of the Abbey some time in the 1170s. It tells the story of a blacksmith in the village of Montacute in Somerset who had a series of visions telling him to lead the people of the village to the top of a hill and dig for buried treasure. They duly followed the smith to the top of the hill and found a 'large stone cross' buried beneath a rock. They called the lord of the manor, Tovi, a chief advisor to King Cnut, who sought spiritual guidance on where the cross should be placed. It was loaded onto a cart pulled by 'twelve red oxen and twelve white cows'. A priest prayed to the Holy Spirit and Tovi named various suitable locations for the cross – London, Canterbury, Winchester. When he had exhausted nearly all options he thought of the small building he was constructing at Waltham. At the mention of its name the cart instantly took off followed by a joyous procession, with people being cured of illnesses along the way.

Tovi decided to decorate the cross. Upon attempting to nail jewels to its bars 'blood gushed from the stone' further adding to its mystical allure. He dedicated himself to the worship of the cross as did Harold Godwinson, later to become King Harold. Harold rebuilt the church in 1060 and invited Edward the Confessor among the nobles to attend the dedication. Also present was Harold's brother Tostig who lived at Leyton. Harold stopped by the cross on his way from defeating the Norwegians at Stamford Bridge to confront William of Normandy at Hastings. He prayed to the cross and two priests from the Abbey followed him to Hastings to return his body to Waltham should he fall in battle, as he did. They pleaded with William for the body who took pity on them and there was a macabre scene as they picked through the carnage of mutilated bodies unable to identify Harold relying eventually on his wife Edith Swanneschals to make the identification. His body was carried on a bier back to Waltham attended by not only the English but also Normans, and Harold was laid to rest.

The cross continued to work its miracles and it was this that drew pilgrims from all over the country right through the Middle Ages until the Abbey was dissolved in 1540. What happened to the cross remained a mystery.

Sun Street in Waltham Abbey was deserted as was Market Place where the Romans built their settlement. People have lived on the site around the Abbey for at least 8000 years, Mesolithic flints and Neolithic pottery have been excavated, there was also a Bronze Age community resident here. Harold's 11th century church was only one in a sequence of churches built on the site that most likely began in the 7th century. It is a place of great antiquity. There were a smattering of early evening drinkers propped up outside the Welsh Harp pub with its rickety Tudor beams. The White Witch pagan shop was sadly closed so I went straight into the Abbey. I first approached these doors on the Saturday before Easter when I'd set out to fill in some gaps in the map between Blackhorse Road and Chingford. After skirting Banbury Reservoir I'd been seduced by a footpath leading along the edge of Tottenham Marshes and decided to just keep going till I broke out of London.

I sauntered through the northeastern rust belt. The Arriva bus depot with its seemingly endless line of polished red double-deckers punctuated by a platoon of cyan blue suburban cousins was a transport nerds' nirvana. A former HSBC office block had been pulverised into a mound of white concrete that was whipped up into dust clouds by gusts coming down off the Essex hills.

A silver sign showed how to spot otters, but I think the otters have had it with large construction sites. I was tempted by the second of two enticing tributaries leading westwards away from the Lea Navigation – the meandering waters of the Turkey Brook and the Pymmes Brook seem to hold more mystery than the canalised well-trodden waterway.

My boots became coated in a film of white trail dust. I passed under a subdued M25, a road that for me forever belongs to Iain Sinclair, and checked the score in the late kick-off while surveying Rammey Marsh from the riverbank. A group of Eastern European men were laughing and swilling from cans of lager in the middle of the tall grasses.

I arrived at the Abbey doors just before 8 pm. They were unexpectedly open and I enquired, of the two people stood in the porch, why this was the case. 'It's the Easter Vigil', they said, slightly surprised. I took a look inside then strolled in the last light round the peaceful Abbey gardens, half looking for King Harold's tomb.

On the point of giving up and heading for the nearest pub despite believing that the tomb of the last Saxon king would be hard to miss, I stopped to look at a grave slab with a wreath of conifer and some flowers placed on top. Running my fingers over the stone beside it I traced out the letters HAROLD. It was appropriately English that such a symbolic spot in English history was so modestly commemorated.

Deciding to eschew the pub I slipped in at the back of the Abbey for the beginning of the Easter Vigil. A scattering of around 30 worshippers sat in the gloom, the only illumination coming from two candles behind the altar beneath the stained-glass windows that cast star-shaped patterns of light. The readings from Genesis were done in deep, slow, sombre voices. It was certainly the first time I'd ended a walk at a church service but it seemed to fit. As the reading from Exodus started I calculated that I'd paid my homage and crept back out into the streets to get a pork pie from the Co-op and plodded over the Hertfordshire border in the dark to get the train from Waltham Cross back into the heart of the city.

On this walk to Easneye my luck was out and the Abbey was closed. I was hoping to pick up a token from the gift shop to bless my heathen pilgrimage to the burial mound. So I decided to revisit Harold's tomb instead.

The modesty of Harold's burial site was seductive. The last Saxon King of England had a melancholy ring to it. THE STONE MARKS THE POSITION OF THE HIGH ALTAR BEHIND WHICH KING HAROLD IS SAID TO HAVE BEEN BURIED IN 1066.

When I came here with Bermondsey Joyrider Gary Lammin, dressed in stage gear ready to rock, he told me that it may only be part of Harold that was buried here as the Normans were terrified of Harold's almost supernatural prowess. He was a large man, a relative giant, and rumours persisted for years that he was alive and hiding out in the remote hillsides ready to return and reclaim his kingdom. In Gary's story, the Normans cut his body into bits and scattered them across the country to stop King Harold rising from the dead.

You'd never guess at the huge symbolic importance of the site of Harold's tomb: a few families amble over for a look then wander off to David Beckham's favourite pie and mash shop in the market square. There was definitely something special about Waltham Abbey, whether it is the given significance of Harold's tomb or if it's inherent in the landscape. Maybe all those pilgrims etched something deep into the soil. Or perhaps it was the Cult of David Beckham. Either way it has an undeniable magic. And I needed to break its spell if I had any hope of reaching Easneye.

I picked up the Cornmill Stream that runs parallel to the Crooked Mile. Cornmill Meadow is noted for its damselflies and 'nymphs of dragonflies'. A lush broad meadow stretched out to the Lea. A straight path beckoned, a green tunnel following the Meridian Line that I now realised I'd been walking along almost the entire way from Leytonstone. I had an afternoon tea on the hoof of a disappointing Ginsters pulled pork slice washed down with a can of Stella that I picked up in the Co-op in Waltham Abbey.

The Meridian path ends at Paula Haughey's sculpture Travel and Discovery carved from two granite blocks reclaimed from London Bridge when it was dismantled for sale to American oilman Robert P. McCulloch in 1968. It is possibly the last trace of the London Bridge opened in 1831 still in the UK, the rest having been reconstructed in Arizona, missing two blocks – I wonder if they noticed. A human figure is carved into the side facing down the Meridian Line a sun shooting out long beams about the head, a small slit cut into the midriff, I guess to mimic the way that some long barrows channel shafts of light on the solstices. On the reverse the figure stretches their arms into the sky to grasp a crescent moon flanked by stars. The sides are adorned with what appear to be instruments of navigation and time calculation.

Just as I settled down for a rest on the bench nearby I heard a man calling out the name of his dog. Then a white Jack Russell scampered by, nose to the ground feverishly following a scent. 'Have you lost your dog?', I asked. He looked flustered so I spent the next 5 minutes helping to herd the pooch back onto the path where the man eventually leashed the beast. I spent many childhood Sunday afternoons tracking our Jack Russell with my Dad, once she went to ground in a fox hole and I made the old man go home to fetch a shovel so we could dig her out in the dark.

My focus on the burial mound meant that I bypassed the Royal Gunpowder Mills marked more mysteriously on my OS map as a Government Research Establishment. Officially there'd been no actual research undertaken here since the early 1990s and it now functions as a visitor attraction. Explosives were produced on the site for over 300 years starting in 1660, in the postwar period switching to rocket propellants with the growth of the Mills running in parallel with the fortunes of the British Empire – from powder for the cannons used in the Second Anglo-Dutch War to the liquid fuelled rocket engines of cold war cruise missiles. Now it was largely covered by alder woodland and a heronry.

I skirted the edge of a large heavy ploughed field and startled a massive pigeon in the hedgerow, the sudden loud clatter of its wings taking flight making me jump out of my skin in turn. A rabbit rose from its hiding place and scuttled over a grassy bank and I basked in the early evening sun. There's no finer place to be at this time of day than in a field just outside the edge of London, although I started to seriously doubt whether I could cover the last seven miles in the two hours of remaining sunlight. Such was the therapeutic effect of the sunlight and scenery that I wasn't overly concerned at this point, still in the grip of the journey.

A track at Fishers Green – the point at which pilgrims bound from Waltham to Walsingham would have branched off for Saffron Walden and Newmarket – brought me to my first contact with the river, at the point where the Cornmill Stream has its confluence with the Horsemill Stream not long after it has conjoined with the Old River Lea. Pagans worshipped the confluence of rivers and streams making votive offerings, the glorious Battersea Shield being a famous example, found at the point where the Thames and Effra meet. Whatever treasure lay lurking beneath the silt here may have been buried by the culverting of the watercourse as it progressed into the Flood Relief Channel.

I looked across at the broad waters of Turnershill Marsh and south towards home – the Lea providing a direct physical link to Leyton then up along the now submerged Philly Brook to my front door. Through the tall stalks of bankside reeds I saw Viking boats cruising up to their stronghold at Ware. They would have heard the same birdsong that filled the air around me – looked out across the marshes at an alien land there for the taking. On summer evenings on these marshy stretches of the upper Lea, you gain a sense of walking through time: narrowboats, long boats, the royal barges of Elizabeth I making her way to Waltham Abbey, only the pylons act as an intrusion. Otters had made their homes around the Seventy Acres Lakes, digging their holts into the soft banks around the network of islands. Bitterns patrolled the skies. Kingfishers observed from their waterside perches. Coots, moorhens, and cormorants soundtracked the scene.

I rested on a carved bench-sculpture hybrid on Holyfield Marsh listening to the low throb of an electricity substation. The marsh takes it name from the medieval nunnery that was linked to Waltham Abbey. Perceval writes of 'nightly revels between the monks of Waltham and the fair inmates of the Cheshunt nunnery'. He recounted a prank played by one of the favourites of Henry VIII who set up a kind of deer trap, a 'buckstall' on the marshes, perhaps where I was sitting on a strip of land between the marshes and the river. 'When the monks issued from the nunnery with some of the "obliging" nuns, a great noise was suddenly made behind them', and they were chased into the traps. In the morning they were presented to Henry who found the scene hilarious and declared, 'he had often seen sweeter, but never more beautiful, or fatter venison'. It all sounds like the plot of a Carry On film.

Sitting in the evening sun it hit me that I wouldn't make it to Easneye that day – I'd woefully underestimated the distance from Sewardstone and my own dawdling, sucking in the ambience. I pulled out my pocket camera and confessed a sense of despair. A couple holding hands crunched past on the gravel path and barely glanced my way – a person talking to a camera at arms length was hardly an unusual sight these days, far more common than an otter sliding through the water. I felt sick in my gut – a failed journey. Was it a sign that I should abandon the entire project, I asked myself. I'd spent the summer planning this walk and trying to wangle the time from family responsibilities to make my pilgrimage only to fall short. Even conjuring the mental image of the lustful monks and nuns, cassocks all ruffled in that deer trap couldn't cheer me up.

I had recently read Iain Sinclair's Black Apples of Gower before interviewing him about this and his London Overground book. One line particularly stuck from Black Apples, jotted down in my notebook not for the interview but to ponder on: 'The walks that truly haunt, and hurt, are the ones that walk you'. Was this one of those walks? It started to feel that way as I made my way onto the towpath of the Lea Navigation – the quest reduced to the status of a stroll. Another of Sinclair's books, American Smoke, that I'd read earlier in the year, raised the notion of the 'bad journey' as he travelled down the West Coast of America on the trail of the Beats and associated poets. A 'bad journey' to Mexico led to the death of Neal Cassady, the Beat icon of Kerouac's On The Road; Nazi architect Albert Speer pacing out a transcontinental trek in the yard of Spandau Prison; Lew Welch walking into the redwood forest of Gary Snyder's retreat in California never to be seen again. When Sinclair visited Snyder in his hideaway the old Beat Buddhist poet asked Sinclair how Epping Forest is doing. This felt like my own 'bad journey' from the Forest along the Lea – but at least it wouldn't kill me, hopefully.

Two joggers jolted me from my introspection by asking directions to Turnford College. I uncrumpled my OS map and pointed to where it sat beneath Hell Wood, and they jogged off in the wrong direction. I plodded on with no actual destination, just walking till the end of daylight.

At Nazeing I passed two narrow boats moored by the towpath – the first was named Odin, the next Odyssey – Odin's Odyssey, what did that mean? The fusion of two myths. I was looking for signs telling me to carry on with the journey, if not today then later. Maybe I was clutching at straws. Another sign could emerge later from the teasels.

At Broxbourne I had the option of a train back to London but opted instead to join the New River Path. I'd often walked the short stretch through Canonbury to Stoke Newington so was curious about its upper reaches. This too was a link to a more obscure myth – that of Merlin's Cave at Penton Mound in Islington where the New River ends beneath a covered reservoir, and the colourful stories spun by Elizabeth Gordon of a London dominated by four sacred prehistoric mounds.

The New River passed through Hoddesdon where coinage issued by the Iron Age chieftain Cunobelinus was excavated. Dubbed 'King of the Britons' by the Roman historian Suetonius, he is the Cymbeline of Shakespeare's play.

The path is thick with midges. A vandalised portaloo lies on its side in the trees spilling its filth onto the soil. The only people I see are a Polish couple swilling cans of lager from a black plastic bag hung from the railing – reminding me that I still had an empty can of Stella in my bag.

If the journey was to be incomplete this final peaceful stretch of the New River was a decent consolation as I passed Victorian pumping stations and allotments. The sunset painted orange zig-zags across the water around the dark patches of weed. By the time I reached Rye House the cadmium sunset had been sucked into the water rendering it a river of fire.

As I sloped into the Rye House pub next to the station, Journey's Don't Stop Believing blared out of the sound system. I'd been look-ing for a sign – maybe this was it, delivered via a West Coast rock anthem in an empty pub on the banks of the River Lea. Don't Stop Believing. If I had any doubts the following tune was Running Up That Hill by Kate Bush telling me to make my way up the high ground to the Easneye burial mound on a hill overlooking the Lea. I decided to disregard Katy Perry's California Gurls that came on next as I sat in the garden by the river – lord knows what that was telling me.

CHAPTER 9

THE ROAD TO EASNEYE – ST MARGARET'S TO THE MOUND

In the period after the failed walk to Easneye I fell into a slump – nothing as grand as a depression but more like a simmering malaise, a few stops short of what Alan Partridge called being 'clinically fed up'. In search of a palliative, I decided to pick up the journey where I'd left off and calculated that it could just about be done between dropping the kids off at school and picking them up at home time.

Whenever I chose a day for the expedition to resume, something managed to get in the way – a couple of hours' work that needed to be done, a trip to the vet, a dental appointment for my youngest son, a hangover. My sleep pattern took a walk on the wild side, I was going to bed at 4 or 5am then up again at 7.30am for the school run – so that the only useful action I could complete during the day would be as an extra in a zombie movie (as long they were the old-fashioned slow zombies). As the days shortened, weekends became about building up a sleep bank and I would awake after midday realising I'd missed the opportunity to head off up the Lea Valley.

Despite all this, the Mound wouldn't leave me. I was invited to take part in two public discussions on the current state of London on the basis of my ongoing video documentation of campaigns to save estates and precious public assets. On each occasion, I found myself sitting there in front of a large earnest audience somehow segueing in a mention of the Mounds at Pinehurst and Easneye, wrong-footing and perplexing my fellow panellists. I had a mantra running through my head: 'Don't mention the Mounds, Don't mention the Mounds', like Basil Fawlty desperately trying not to mention the war in front of his German guests. The more I tried to hold it in, the more it expelled forth with gusto. What was going on? Don't Stop Believing, that cheesy rock anthem had become my unofficial personal theme tune: had it cursed me or was it leading me?

I was still ruined in the mornings, looking out at clear skies thinking it would be the perfect day to finally ascend the hill to Easneye mound but unthinkable after three hours sleep. It would never happen, I should give it up. I stuck to journeys closer to home – Mayesbrook Park in Barking, Diwali in Trafalgar Square with my son, the old lanes from Fleet Street down to the Thames then up over the buried rivers of the Fleet and the Walbrook. Morning crawls around Soho streets being hosed down and up around Kings Cross watching the guts being slowly ripped out of the heart of London, surgically removed a block at a time. The iconic pizzeria opposite the Scala Cinema closed and soon to be bulldozed was one of the saddest sights of that time.

A new upstairs section opened in my favourite morning coffee haunt where I could retreat further into a corner performing rites of caffeine necromancy. Slumped there one day in the pit of the malaise, I was reading Umberto Eco's The Mysterious Flame of Queen Loana, and a phrase jumped out at me: 'You can only anticipate the future if you can call the past to mind'. I read it several times. Was this why the Mound had become so important to me?

One Saturday night in December, feeling ill, I crashed out early. There'd been an event in Leytonstone earlier that day celebrating the area's link to Stuart Freeborn, who'd created the iconic character designs for the Star Wars movies. Apparently, he partly modelled Yoda on his own face. Perhaps the excitement of following Darth Vader and a gang of Stormtroopers along Grove Green Road with the kids had taken its toll.

I awoke at 6am on the Sunday morning feeling terrible. The family were sound asleep. I popped a couple of paracetamol and realised that I could finally make it out to Easneye, why else had I mysteriously woken up at this hour when for months I had only just turned in at this time. I briefly considered deferring the trip until the solstice: a nice idea but, tempered by the reality that my sleep pattern could well return to its nocturnal cycle by then, I decided to carry on.

The dog sloped in to say hello while I checked the maps, sniffed my leg then returned to its bed. I pulled up the blind and peered out at the dark, wet streets.

By 7.30am I was on my way to the station in the freezing cold drizzle. Something about the mounds in the upper Lea Valley had been with me since June and I needed to finally lay it to rest at Easneye even if it meant spending the rest of the week in bed. I took the remainder of the paracetamol and picked up some Nurofen at the station.

There was a grey smudge of first light as the train pulled out of Liverpool Street. A group of Irish railway workers sat in the adjacent seats fresh off a night shift recounting quantities that'd been shifted along the tracks. Lights glowed in the LCC estates as we glided through Hackney. We faded through the giant building site that was once Stratford, the perpetual construction schemes forming the real Olympic legacy – a safe dumping ground for dubious overseas investments, flats that will never be lived in, office spaces gleamingly bare. The illuminated skyscrapers glimmered through a kind of Shanghai smog that only blankets E15 and E20.

The train then shadowed my walk out to Rye House. I spotted locations passed on that sun-blessed September day. The misty marsh landscape, red pools worthy of their own pilgrimages. I surrendered to the slight insanity of my quest that felt essential, deep in my core. The two locations, the Olympic Park and the Easneye Mound, linked by the River Lea, a thread of power, as they were when the Bronze Age barrows were erected. Ormsby's tantalising theory that a pre-Romano British line of communication ran along the western edge of the Lea Valley linking Stratford to Ware and Hertford then onto the Catuvellauni citadel north of what became Roman Verulam. The ancient infrastructure of London, still the key to centres of influence – the lower Lea development the engine of so much of what was happening in London.

I began to view these mounds and earthworks as the physical remnants of some of the first attempts to raise structures that became the city we now live in – and in a way symbolising lines of power that still exert themselves on the city. My obsession was all part of trying to understand what was happening in London at that moment, and I thought some of the answer to that question may just lie in a wood in Hertfordshire.

The other possibility was that I was entering the grip of a midlife crisis. They were not mutually exclusive.

I disembarked at a cold and dreary St Margaret's station just before 9am. The Irish railwaymen stayed on the train presumably to Ware or Hertford, the end of the line. The level crossing and the cooing wood pigeons cast a rustic air. Over the beautiful stone bridge across the Lea I paused letting the rain hit my face, and looked south to Rye Marshes where the Rye House Plotters allegedly planned to ambush and murder the Catholic King James I on his way back from Newmarket races. Regicide was very much on the table in 17th century England, the beheading of Charles I still fresh in the mind. Whether the plot ever existed in reality or not, or if it was a ruse to eliminate the opposition, conspirators were rounded up, tortured and executed and another corrupt regime lumbered on for a mere three years more before it was swept away by the so called 'Glorious Revolution'. The river flowed on regardless, aloof to our piffling follies and the changing fortunes of monarchs. It saw Boudicca pass through astride a chariot on her way to torch London, and the eddies swirled, reeds swayed, and fish lurked in the weeds as they always did, and still do today.

Smoke rose from the cottages along the High Street of Stanstead Abbotts. Christmas lights twinkled in the windows and on the lampposts. The village slept and I didn't blame it, even the newsagent appeared to be closed.

Stanstead Abbotts is as old as its name suggests, recorded in the Domesday book and doubtless stretching back to earlier times given its prominent position by the River Lea. The local historical society wrote that the village fell within the tribal area of the Catuvellauni whose territory spread across Hertfordshire, Bedfordshire, and parts of Cambridgeshire, in the centuries either side of the Roman conquest.

A blackboard advertising Christmas party bookings was slumped against a red and gold bollard outside the 17th century Red Lion pub. That'd be a good place to end the walk beside the pub's roaring fire, although a Costa Coffee in Ware was more likely.

Glorious morning birdsong scored the turning out of the village along what I hoped was the final leg of the approach to Easneye. These damp chill winter mornings in the weeks before Christmas made me think of my Dad heading off with his shotgun folded inside his wax jacket to take advantage of any stray pheasants. The old man had an uneasy truce with the local farmers and game-keepers where he seemingly roamed the fields and woods at total liberty, dawn and dusk. This memory jolts me to give him a call and I narrate the scene along Capel Road with the flat fields leading down to the Lea and the steep banks rising to woodland and fields behind the flint church of St Andrews. 'The pheasants won't fly in this weather', he says, 'so you can get up close'. There's not enough of a country boy left in me (was there ever) to even contemplate snapping the neck of an earthbound pheasant, but the old chap's hunting tips brought me to the entrance of All Nations Easneye College.

A road led up past a redbrick gatehouse to Thomas Fowell Buxton's Easneye House, home to trainee missionaries since 1964. The house had starred as the notorious St Trinian's School for Girls just a decade before in the classic Ealing Comedy. Thomas Fowell Buxton bought the 3000-acre site that takes in a sweep of the surrounding countryside to build a house for his 11 children. He and his wife Hannah Gurney had 14 children in total but 3 died during infancy. Some of the Buxton children are buried in Leytonstone churchyard. The house was a considerable step up from the already grand house at Leytonstone where he'd lived for 18 years after taking it over from his brother Edward North Buxton MP, author of the still essential Epping Forest guidebook. It was even further away from the house in Brick Lane attached to the Truman Brewery where Thomas and Hannah had spent the first two years of married life. It was a statement of his position of power and influence – and, as I've touched on before, the Buxton-Gurneys were ridiculously influential as a family. Hannah's father, Samuel Gurney, was known as 'the Banker's Banker' and she had grown up in Ham House, the grounds of which now form West Ham Park. One of her brothers was an MP and two of Thomas's siblings also had seats in the House of Commons. Of their 11 children raised here at Easneye, Geoffrey Fowell Buxton became director of Barclays Bank (which was formed by a merger with the family's Gurney's Bank), John Henry who opened the mound with his father that morning in 1899, followed his Dad into the beer trade and became Director of Truman's Brewery, and Alfred Buxton was the Chair of London County Council. They were a one-family Illuminati.

Thomas commissioned Manchester architect Alfred Waterhouse, most famous for designing the Natural History Museum, to build them a grand gothic pile – which he paid for in cash, no mortgage required even though that would hardly have been an issue when your father-in-law owns a bank.

The gatehouse at the bottom of the lane was like a miniaturised version of the mansion, an architectural appetiser for visitors. I considered bowling up to the house and seeing if I could go through the grounds to the mound but decided against it, preferring a furtive scrambling through the woods. My mound quest needed the cherry topping of a potential act of trespass.

The muddy path leading in the direction of the tumulus doubled as a public bridleway. A rabbit skipped through the overgrown bank that separated the closely cropped college grounds from a field of winter greens. The steep path quickly rendered me short of breath, the illness biting in, but the peaceful misty morning induced an uplifting feeling of release. The Lea Valley pylons were just visible in the distance. I realised that it was three months to the day since I first set out from Leytonstone heading here, and now the crest of the hill was within view and hopefully the mound.

I spotted a ridge running near the track with a semi-circular ditch and faint path leading into the trees. An earthbound pheasant hopped and shuffled through the leaves, just as my Dad predicted. I tried to align the OS map with the digital map on my phone to confirm my location. It all seemed to agree. This must be it, I thought, the site of the Easneye Mound.

I excitedly scrambled over wet, slippery foliage up the outer bank, ascending what I believed to be the barrow excavated by Thomas Fowell Buxton, John Henry Buxton, and Sir John Evans on 19th July 1899.

'The barrow, which is situated about a quarter of a mile to the north-east of Easneye House, is in the midst of a wood, and is not laid down on the Ordnance Map on the scale of six inches to a mile.'

J Evans 1900

The summit was marked out with blue plastic stakes and a large

146

wooden drum supported on poles wrapped in lengths of shredded plastic sat in the middle – a curious tribute, perhaps there to demarcate the location. The guns of the pheasant shoot started to crack in the distance but by then I was in a reverie of amateur archaeology stepping back into that grainy photo in the pamphlet. ''It is about sixty feet in diameter at the base, and its summit is about ten feet above the level of the neighbouring ground.'

I circled the base of the mound to match the size to Evans' description, looking back to the summit to check the height, circling the perimeter, and became certain that this was the Easneye barrow that'd stalked me for six months, inhabited my dreams, interrupted conversations, becoming an obsession.

Walking through Shadwell with Iain Sinclair shooting for our film of his book London Overground, he raised the topic of my fascination with the Lea Valley mounds and asked what I had gleaned from my activities working with London housing campaigners. All I could manage by way of answer at the time was that both gave me hope. Evans again:

'I was, at first, in hope that, on examination, it would prove to be of Roman date, and analogous in character with the Youngsbury Barrow, about three miles to the north, opened in 1899, of which I have given an account in the Archaeologica, vol. lii, p287. These hopes were to be disappointed.'

Bare tree trunks reached into the grey sky. A scattering of pine trees – there's a lone pine tree growing out of the top of the mound in the Buxton photo. It's possible these pine trees were around when the mound was opened – if only they could talk. They'd probably be more inclined to tell the story of the American P51 MK 1 Mustang that crashed into Easneye Wood in October 1942. The crash was witnessed by a young Leslie R Miller who recounted the incident in 1993 and the story was later published by the Stanstead Abbotts historical society.

'Two North American P51 MK1 Mustangs roared at roof top height over my home, much to my delight, but little knowing that a tragedy was only seconds away for one of the aircraft. Both were flying on a northerly heading along the Lea Valley where just a half mile ahead loomed the edge of Easneye Woods rising some 150 feet above the floor of the valley. It was to spell doom to the starboard Mustang which at first clipped the treetops and then was dragged down further into the mass of trees until it disintegrated upon contact with the larger tree trunks. It was stated at the time that the pilot was catapulted from the aircraft and impaled on the bough of a tree, although so far I have not been able to verify this. He was however killed when the aircraft impacted.'

Millar recorded how he later discovered that the Mustangs had become disorientated in poor visibility while returning to their airfield in Sawbridgeworth, a little further northeast, in Hertfordshire. He returned to Easneye Woods in the early 1990s and retrieved wreckage from the plane buried in the undergrowth.

I made my way back to the centre of the mound to survey the scene. Raindrops splattered the leaves. Shrill pheasant calls punctured the damp air. On the other side of the River Ash the distant pop of the shoot heralded the fall of their comrades.

'As the centre was approached traces of burning became evident inasmuch as numerous small fragments of charcoal were found, and eventually beneath a slab of partially charred wood a considerable deposit of burnt bones was discovered.'

J Evans

I could almost see Thomas Fowell and his son John Henry Buxton digging into the mound in 1899, with Evans stood observing, taking notes, hoping for a rich hoard of Roman artefacts to be unearthed. But there was not a single piece of pottery or metal, and they had to be satisfied with the jawbone of a young pig.

Slumbering under my feet were the charred remains of a Bronze Age chieftain. As Dave Binns pointed out across the Lea Valley at the Pinehurst Mound, these burials were reserved for a newly emergent ruling class that evolved from the more egalitarian societies that preceded them. Whatever else they were saying to their contemporaries, these tumuli left a mark on the landscape that thousands of years later says to us 'I was here' like graffiti carved into a tree trunk. And here I was, drawn out of London to this spot on a cold, damp Sunday morning before Christmas, finding it difficult to pull myself away. The job was done, I had found the Buxton Mound, I could just turn around and get home before lunchtime but for some reason I lingered. Crows joined the pheasants in song, cawing from the highest boughs. It felt like a sacred place. The people who constructed this tumulus chose this spot for a reason, its commanding views eastwards perhaps, its position high up on the ridge above the river valley. Or was there some other less practical significance they projected onto this landscape?

An article on the Stanstead Abbotts Local History Society website by Ron Dale refers to the 'Sacred Groves of Easneye'. Apparently, medieval charters mention 'Alwine's Frith' at Easneye, a 'Frith' being an Anglo-Saxon word for a place (or state) of peace, sanctuary, and asylum. Dale explores the various meanings of the word and how it was associated with sacred groves and pre-Christian pagan worship. It's interesting to think that the significance of this high wooded outcrop had passed on down through the ages from one group of settlers to the next, and was finally even venerated by the Quaker Buxton family.

'The bones and ashes were, after examination, placed in an earthenware jar, with an inscription on a copper plate stating when and by whom the barrow was opened, and what was found in it. The jar, with its contents, was then placed in the centre of the mound, where the bones were discovered, and the earth was replaced in the excavation.'

J Evans

I finally wrenched myself away – I'd found my sanctuary, discovered a place of peace in this turbulent time, vindicated to have finally seen this crazed quest through to completion.

CHAPTER 10

BEATING THE BOUNDS WITH IAIN SINCLAIR

S omebody once posed the question, 'Why did the psychogeog-
rapher cross the road?'. 'I don't know', I answered, 'but when
they got there, they discovered Iain Sinclair had already written
about it'. Sinclair is the London magus, the keeper of its magic
and its secrets and it was a privilege to be out walking with him.
Tramping his old turf on this one particular day when we were
making a film based on his book London Overground, 'dowsing
for the railway' as it disappeared underground between Shadwell
and Wapping. With the camera rolling talking about the situation in London he asked me where I saw hope and optimism. We
were walking down Sutton Street, Shadwell past a fine redbrick
London county council estate. Iain continued, 'my own sense of
having done this journey round the Overground is that it is a kind
of "last London", we've lost one kind of organic city that existed
for hundreds or thousands of years and it's really become something quite new and strange and in some ways interesting now,
but different'.

I told Iain about some of the campaigns I'd witnessed and documented and how that strength of community gave me hope that the soul of London would survive this assault. He'd seen the same spirit of resistance in his own corner of the city, where a campaign had seen off a threat to the beloved Ridley Road Market in Dalston. Iain had collaborated with one of the key figures in that campaign, local lawyer Bill Parry-Davis, who is also a mean jazz saxophonist. Bill had walked us around the Dalston redevelopment zone, explaining how the Dalston Square development had spawned the model of selling off to overseas buyers that had become a feature of many schemes across the city.

'Shadwell's a significant point of transit as commuters from Dalston and Hackney pick up the DLR into Docklands, demographics overlapping', Iain says surveying the terrain ahead. We were covering a relatively small area from Shadwell station down to the Thames and looping back. This part of East London is littered with evidence of Anglo-Saxon settlement recorded in the place names. Blida's corner becomes Bethnal Green, Stibba's land at Stepney, and Waeppa's encampment at Wapping. Shadwell is said to be derived from 'shallow well'. This was an earlier new London that slowly rose from the marshlands and gravel terraces spreading east of the Roman wall that was protecting the deserted colonial outpost.

We crossed Cable Street, site of one of London's most important battles, when Oswald Moseley's Blackshirts were defeated by a coalition of dockers, Jews, communists, trade unionists, and the ordinary folk of East London. We ducked through the heavy vehicles of another building project as we approached and turned onto the Highway, 'The Shard is really there like a dagger', Iain says over the auditory assault of thunderous traffic. The Highway is the most likely location for Waeppa's original settlement before the drainage of the marshes and the establishment of 'Wapping on the woze' (or mud).

'Feels to me like the city's becoming very fragmented, a series of blocks that are hard to connect up. Once upon a time when I was working down here as a gardener in the '70s then things like the Hawskmoor churches were real markers in the territory. Now they're being dwarfed by other structures that have grown up all round them and that sense of a pattern isn't really here anymore in the same way', Iain riffed as we walked along the Highway.

The territory that Iain so vividly captured in his books was a zone in transition as the docks moved further east along the Thames and the planners and speculators moved in. I suppose the challenge now is to find a new pattern in this emergent city of looming towers and seemingly impenetrable blocks. The psycho-geography of the city evolves as the built environment once again renews and mutates. Our task is to put an ear to the ground and listen to the whispers, record the changes and decode the new con-figurations as they bubble to the surface.

'As you've found in your diggings around, you go back to the re-ally old stuff ... the earthworks, Iron Age settlements, relics, altars of a culture way beyond even the idea of the settlement of a city. And that gives you a lift in terms of living with what we've got now', Iain continued, referencing my journeys in the Lea Valley, the breath billowing out of his mouth in the freezing January air, the Thames getting closer.

'It's a kind of solace really', I said. 'I think it's actually partly a search for understanding as well because of the visible remains of when people seem to have started to put down markers, you know, physical markers. Obviously there were things before that. So it's almost like a way of going back to the very beginning. And look-ing at it from there. Particularly when I went up to Easneye just before Christmas, which overlooks the Lea and Widbury hillfort, two places that are quite close together and I would never really have connected those places to London. But then you see that they were part of a culture that spans the Lea Valley and out to the edge of northwest Essex.'

I wanted to know what Iain thought of the idea that the Lea Valley was a historic generator of change in London. He'd been a prominent early critic of the London Olympic project. He had a long history with the area, working as a day labourer at Chobham Farm, Stratford in the early 1970s. Events to promote his book Ghost Milk, published in 2011, which contained chapters on the preparations for London 2012, were banned from buildings owned by Hackney council, as an official Olympic Borough.

'The Lea Valley is so difficult,' Iain replied. 'I'd been avoiding lots of elements of the Lea Valley for a long time. When I went back to the old sewage outfall and started to pick my way around there the other day, there was just a sense of it being overwhelmingly narrated. That there's a story being imposed on you and the canal bank is just so blocked up with joggers who are listening to their soundtracks and people cycling along furiously. It's really quite difficult to just even move through the landscape. And all the time, the fences and the hoardings are just covered with this mass of material. Stories of futures that they want this landscape to become, so it's written in advance rather than growing as it used to, bit by bit, piecemeal. It's like inventing a completely new city. As if it were a huge clearance of Amazonian forests.'

I wondered if the regeneration around the Lea Valley was integral to the pattern of development Iain had documented along the recently created London Overground network. Back in the 1990s when the North London Line was threatened with closure, it was argued in an academic paper by Jerram and Wells, that investment in the railway could help regenerate the East by providing a 'major tourist and leisure asset'.

'Yes. It's a model,' Iain replied. 'Thing with the Overground is to try and colonise and remake a geography that is a spin-off and a satellite of the major developments that happened in the Stratford hub. You've created that using the smokescreen of enormous amounts of public money and media attention that could be whipped up around the fraudulent Olympics over a short period of time. That's just a sleight of hand to carry forward this setting up of the huge shopping mall of Westfield and all of the building development that could be sold off in blocks to the Chinese or whatever.

'And then the Olympics have to be serviced, so the railways have to be changed in different ways and you make this Overground circuit right round London, which creates a microclimate biased towards certain forms of regeneration and development, with the actual physical spaces of the railway beneath it being gradually given over to shopping hubs and retail hubs. And it's not in any way to service the people who live around these areas. It's entirely to do with a form of retail tourism, bussed in from outside. Doesn't actually bring anything of benefit to the area. And yet it's using up money given to the council to regenerate after the riots. I see that as a pattern for what's happening around the whole span of where we're going today.'

We walked down Garnet Street crossing the giant iron bridge that spans one end of Shadwell Basin. The street names record the goods that flowed into the city, their aromas filling the air – Cinnamon Street, Wine Close, Spirit Quay, Vinegar Street, Brewhouse Lane. Wapping High Street was once the frontline of the new London.

'I can remember vividly what happened down here in Docklands ... Well, the riverside reaches, which was the classic of these great buildings that had been warehouses along the working river. First of all, being taken on by artists and people with a real sense of attachment to the beauty and the life of the area, and then obviously turning into up-market purchases for people who are working in the banking sector in Docklands itself. And so you then just create this huge dormitory zone which again loses its connection with what was here originally.'

Wandering these dark empty streets were some of my first experiences of London in the late '80s, a student from Bucks seeking out parties in the flats that were being rented out on the cheap after the property market crashed. It was an uncanny dead quarter, a vacant movie set yet to be allocated a script. I'd been told that some of the key movers in the Docklands redevelopment had been enrolled to advise on the plans for Stratford City and the Olympic Legacy. It was no accident that the themes were being repeated.

We carefully descended the slippery stone steps of Wapping Old Stairs, an ancient right of way to the riverside dating back to the Middle Ages. Standing on the beach beneath Tower Bridge, the Gherkin and the Shard, challengers on the skyline shimmer in the distance. I produce a battered old paperback edition of Downriver, Iain's prophetic 1991 book, that not only brilliantly nailed the Thatcherite Docklands carve up, but predicted the new London. Standing on the low-tide Thames mud Iain reflected on the transition that has happened since.

'It's a different city to Downriver' he tells me. 'Downriver was the height of the Thatcherite period, when all of the stuff that's happening now was there like a whisper from the future, and the book tried to pick up on that. But now we're living in what that anticipated. I was being satirical about the idea of a return to the prison hulks and the barges and the privatised prisons. But this actually has become fact.'

We made our way back up Wapping Old Stairs to the High Street where Iain disappeared through an iron gate into St John's Churchyard, one of those odd survivors in a torrent of change, repurposed as a public park. We're drawn to the heritage plaque on a high brick wall that Iain had missed on his previous trampings.

'Thomas Rainsborough buried in the churchyard on the 14th of November, 1648 after a funeral procession organised by the Leveller movement. Rainsborough was a spokesman for the Levellers and a colonel in the New Model Army. Killed by a Royalist raiding party during the siege of Pontefract. On the day of the funeral, a Leveller leaflet recorded the inscription on Rainsborough's tomb. It proclaimed Rainsborough had made "Kings, lords, commoners, and judges shake, cities and committees quake." He was, it said, "just, valiant, and true" and it ended with the words that here Rainsborough "bids the noble Levellers adieu". Plaque unveiled by Cllr Rania Khan, writer John Rees, and politician Tony Benn in 2013.'

I wondered if omissions from Iain's record such as this created an anxiety in the writer of a city with its multiple layers and ever-shifting sands – could he ever produce a definitive version of even just one walk? He laughed at the suggestion that such a thing should even be thought possible. 'The city is a series of these psychic mappings that reinforce our own identity. And then once you've written about them, even casually, you have to come back to them. So you keep repeatedly returning to the ground, it's no longer the ground necessarily just of London, but it's the ground of your own version of London. And so adding to that story is only beneficial. I don't feel that the first version is now illegitimate. I now feel that actually it's gained something by the instinct of being here and discovering much later that one of the Levellers is buried here.' And with that we exited the churchyard back into the streets of Wapping, me trailing Iain as I stopped to gather cutaways of the churchyard for the film.

The light in Watts Street moved Iain to think of Francis Bacon, a figure spotted at the bus stop in the 1980s.

'When Francis Bacon got his house on Narrow Street, he couldn't paint at all because the light was too live. So he had to go back to

Kensington and draw the curtains and have an electric light bulb. Get out the photos and all the mess and paint there. And he just came down here because he wanted to be close to what was left of the Dockers. I used to see him at the bus stop every day when I was gardening around St Anne's.'

The Wapping light also drew the great JMW Turner who inherited two cottages in Watts Street which he converted into a pub. Here he installed one of his mistresses as landlady and conducted a secret life adopting her name for cover. We stood outside the Old Star looking up at the smeared image of Turner on the pub sign, now renamed Turner's Old Star. 'Once you pass Tower Bridge everything is possible, everything is permitted', Iain mused.

We found ourselves back on this terrain four years later, almost by accident, fulfilling Iain's prophecy of the return to the same ground you've walked before. I'd made a video of a walk tracing footsteps laid down in WG Sebald's Austerlitz, with the artist Bob and Roberta Smith. We'd followed instructions Iain had given us and used the chapter of his book The Last London describing the walk as a guide. When he saw the film, Iain offered to take me on an alternative route of overlapping narratives – part of Van Gogh's London, sites in the City of London associated with his recent trip to Peru, and Emmanuel Swedenborg's grave which somehow linked to Sebald's novel.

We met outside WH Smith at Liverpool Street Station, once part of the opulent Great Eastern Hotel. Among Iain's many casual jobs in the past, he'd worked night shifts at the station as a baggage handler, in the days when it was a dark and dingy terminus, as described in Austerlitz. We moved on quickly through the City breaching London Wall, then diving into Austin Friars Passage off Great Winchester Street. Iain touched the 'pregnant' wall in the alleyway: 'You actually can put your hand on it, avoiding the chewing gum, and you take the temperature of another era of London', he said. 'Taking the temperature' of London is a good description of Iain Sinclair's work. He's had an amazing knack for finding the territory that contains the story of London at that particular time. The Thatcher era in Downriver, the mid-90s end of Tory rule in Lights Out for the Territory, the early bravado Blair years at the turn of the millennium with London Orbital, through to the new city being spun out of the Overground railway with London Overground. Today we'd be slicing across these timelines ending back with one of Iain's earliest works, Lud Heat, where he accidentally gave birth to a particular Anglo-Celtic variation of psychogeography while working as a gardener in the churchyards of the East End.

After clocking off the locations relating to Van Gogh and the Peru Corporation of London we found ourselves by the Thames at old Billingsgate Market. Passing through the tourists laying siege to the Tower of London, I raised the legend of Bran the Blessed and the alignments linked by myth laid out in EO Gordon's book, Prehistoric London, its Mounds and Circles (1904). According to Gordon's wonderfully romantic mythology of the city, the Tower of London stood on one of its sacred mounds. A sketch map sits inside the cover illustrating these four nodal points.

We retraced our steps through Wapping from the Overground walk, checking in again on the Thomas Rainsborough memorial and Turner's Old Star which had since acquired a new plaque: 'Site of Witchcraft – Lydia Rogers found guilty of allowing the devil to draw blood from her hand to form an evil pact. Confessed her crimes to a minister 1658.' These routes seem destined to continually cross – that's the role of the walker, to stay in perpetual motion traipsing around the city documenting, noting, remembering, keeping a record.

Crossing the Highway, the spire of St George in the East lanced the East End sky, designed by Nicholas Hawksmoor and tagged as a key point in the psychogeography of London, largely thanks to Iain's early writings. Intrigued by EO Gordon's alignments of sacred mounds Iain created his own 'occulted mapping of London' linking sites of the churchyards he tended as a gardener and other points of interest. During breaks he delved into the Tower Hamlets Local History Archive to further research these locations finding a wealth of untapped material. This work resulted in a 1975 self-published book Lud Heat, which found its way to the comic book writer Alan Moore via Neil Gaiman some years later. Lud Heat became source material for Moore's bestselling take on the Ripper Murders, From Hell, adapted for the silver screen starring Johnny Depp. It has continued to inspire psychogeographers ever since. Maps such as those produced by EO Gordon and Iain Sinclair provide a vital counterpoint to the surveys and re-namings being drawn up by developers, new schemes of the city erasing the alignments built up over centuries if not millennia, pushing them beneath the ground.

Iain had recounted these overlapping resonances as we'd passed the Local History Archive in the fading winter light. By the time we stood outside the house believed to be the inspiration for Jacques Austerlitz's home in Alderney Road, Stepney, it was pitch black. The house overlooks Britain's oldest Ashkenazi cemetery as described in the book, which opened in 1697. It marks another occluded London. A survivor in an ever-shifting city.

The Overground walk had resumed at Iain's home in Haggerston where he's lived since the late 1960s. He's remained a permanent feature in an area where so much has changed, a still point in time from the days of the large communal houses and squats populated by artists, dreamers, poets, chancers, drifters and dropouts. This culture still existed in Hackney when I washed up on an estate just off Mare Street, newly demobbed from polytechnic in the early '90s. I remember seeing dog-eared copies of Iain's books on windowsills and paperback floor stacks on tours of neighbouring estate flats. While the smart literary set were still encamped over West, Iain was our poet of the East. Now that Maida Vale and Notting Hill had moved to Hackney, Sinclair stood firm and gobbled up the new readers.

The walk to Iain's house took me close to the New Era Estate, memories of that intense period littering the pavement. Our first walks together overlapped with the subsequent campaigns and talk of what was happening took up much of the moving chatter which then found its way into the public conversations we did together around London Overground. The resulting film returned to this ancient thoroughfare for its premiere, further along Kingsland Road at the Rio Cinema in the East End Film Festival. This old Roman road seemed to be linked to much of the action.

This walk though, following the Overground railway from Haggerston to Shadwell, was on more personal terrain for Iain, a passage through the memory grounds. 'Moved into this area in 1968, just up the road there. A friend of mine had got a communal house, so six of us, who'd known each other in Dublin, all moved in together, and we were trying to work in film, we were endlessly pedalling projects, and then split up. One of us went to work at the BBC, editing some Sherlock Holmes project of the moment. Another one, Tom Baker, who'd written Witchfinder General for Mike Reeves, got a gig working on a Hitchcock programme. I was teaching in Walthamstow, teaching film studies, and sending out guerrilla filmmakers all over London to burn away some stock, and we began to explore this area.'

We were walking down Kingsland Road, crossing the canal, again a generator of change in London, two hundred years since it starting reshaping the industrial city. The aim was to stick as close to the railway line as possible as it carved an arc through the East End down to the river.

'It's taken years and years and years to really get to understand, not only the magic of Hackney, but the kind of underlying patterns of energy, disappearing industry, the different communities. And it was only really when I did the book Hackney Rose Red Empire, that I realised how far wrong I'd been about lots of things in the early days.'

Passing beside the railway arches, beer barrels from a micro-brewery are rolled out into the lane and hosed down. The smell of beer and yeast made Iain recall working in the ullage cellar of Truman's Brewery in Brick Lane with the sculptor and writer Brian Catling. He places the micro-breweries alongside sourdough bakers housed in the railway arches as symbols of the new economy spawned by the revived Overground Railway. The car mechanics and body shops replaced by coffee roasters and yoga studios. Although, our walks around the Overground circuit revealed that the old trades of the arches were still alive and well beside the standard bearers of gentrification. Since our walks, Network Rail sold off the railway arches to an American Hedge Fund that instantly hiked the rents placing many of the new cottage industries in serious jeopardy.

A terrain of newbuilds hug the Overground circuit, borrowing names from local history, replacing estates condemned by Hackney council, tenants displaced and decanted, despite colourful, vibrant campaigns that were ultimately unsuccessful. That's a heritage rarely, if ever, recognised in the new developments. Records of the demolition of the 468 homes on the Kingsland Estate and Haggerston West Estate are buried on the internet amongst adverts for the 761 properties that replaced them in the £110 million regeneration project, that according to its own PR, didn't provide a single council home (55% 'affordable', 45% private sale).

Iain's thesis in London Overground was that the newly restored and revived railway circuit, reclaimed from abandoned sections of track and rebranded, had become a symbol of much of the development in post-Olympic London. He saw this as the landscape that told the story of this period in the way that his walk around the M25 for London Orbital spoke of London at the turn of the millennium.

We skirted the edge of the old City with skeletal frames of disputed developments thieving the daylight from the streets of Norton Folgate, narrow streets that once led pilgrims from the Roman road to the Shoreditch Holy Well. Iain showed me the site of RD Laing's Antiuniversity as we dodged through Shoreditch. The writer so heavily associated with this part of London seemed slightly lost in this landscape of the digital start-up, the fulfilment of Nathan Barley's credo of 'self-facilitating media nodes'. The Chris Morris and Charlie Brooker-authored Channel 4 comedy series tanked in 2005 – it looked like poorly judged science fiction at the time, except to the emergent creatives working these East End streets. Ten years later the Overground railway delivered columns of Nathan Barleys to stops at Hoxton and Shoreditch High Street.

Moving on across Brick Lane towards Whitechapel Iain sensed a shift in mood: 'Just coming across from Shoreditch to here on Cheshire Street, it's a different country, and more than anything else in London, essentially, this bridge here, going over the railway, is like going between East Berlin and West Berlin.' It throws up the East End mythology of the Krays, which intersects with lesser-known stories that Iain has helped highlight over the years, such as that of Emanuel Litvinoff, author of Journey Through a Small Planet, who grew up in the area. Iain talks of how Emanuel's half-brother, David Litvinoff, was said to be the inspiration for the gangster in Nic Roeg's classic film Performance, starring Mick Jagger. 'Alexander Baron, who wrote The Lowlife, wrote a book called King Dido, that was about a family that lived right here, on what they call Hare Marsh. So that history is not eradicated, and crossing the railways is like crossing into the old life.'

The view of the chimney of Truman's brewery once again raised the Buxton connection that seems to resonate throughout this story, and followed us on this walk. The Buxtons married into the Truman's brewing business, and witnessing the squalor of the Victorian East End led them to help establish the London Hospital at Whitechapel.

We passed the park where the Yiddish poet Avram Stencl would sit after escaping from Nazi Germany. Iain talked of how he re-imagined this landscape as 'his own holy Jerusalem in exile'. We had to bypass the Crossrail works at Whitechapel into the street market with its rush of colour and life. Iain's commented on the Crossrail development carving its name through the core of London as a 'blockage in London's psychic currents of the most extreme kind, because they feel free to burrow remorselessly underneath and to close off great tranches of territory; road closed, cyclists dismount, pedestrians bugger off'.

In the process of crossing Whitechapel High Street and weaving through the London Hospital we lost our bearings, 'getting creatively lost', and found ourselves in the churchyard of St Dunstan's, Stepney. 'It's nostalgic because this was where I first really started to write about London because I was a gardener in 1974, just across the road there in St George's Fields, and we used to cut the grass here', Iain tells me as he perched on the corner of a giant stone tomb. In the bright late afternoon autumn light it's a welcome moment of calm after 'the frenzy of the railway, and its newbuild developments and its Boris Bikes'. We've left the contemporary concerns of the city for the moment and feel lost outside time somewhere between the mid-1970s and the 950s when Dunstan, Bishop of London, established the first stone church on the site of an older wooden church. Iain says that Dunstan had connections to alchemy, and having been Abbot of Glastonbury carried with him a cartload of associated English mythology up from the southwest.

Sometimes I think of psychogeography, that Iain Sinclair has done more than anyone to popularise, as a coping mechanism in a city that is constantly undergoing a process of disappearance and re-birth. It's cognitive behavioural therapy for the inhabitants of an ever-changing landscape. In the face of the re-writing of the physical environment, it's vital to maintain a landscape of the imagination that we can recognise and relate to. I thought back to my circuit of the Olympic Park with Chris, a resident of Clays Lane, and how he'd struggled to place streets he'd walked every day within the new terrain. His mental map had been involuntarily edited by the planners. You could sense the therapeutic effect of returning to this churchyard in Stepney, outside the developer's claw.

We did seven walks in total for the Overground film, each revealing a different chapter in the story of London, but each now following an overarching theme in its redevelopment. It became like a tour of building sites. Even when we started a southern section on the Thames shoreline in front of St Mary's Church, Battersea, a great new block of reflective glass had been plonked down behind the church dominating a part of the view east. The church where William Blake had married Katherine Boucher, and where Turner would sit and paint the river, had been defiled. The towers marching along the river now dominated stretches of the Thames from Barking to Hammersmith.

Our circuit though had begun in Rotherhithe, Iain accompanied by his companion for the single schlepp recounted in the book, film-maker Andrew Kötting. It was Kötting who'd first inspired me to pick up a camera after seeing his debut feature Gallivant at the Sydney Film Festival in 1997. This lyrical circumnavigation of the coastline of Britain in a camper van spoke directly to my backpacker's heart. The grainy Super8 footage overlaying a cut-up soundtrack of archive voices and music from an undefined era was a postcard from a 'visionary landscape'. I went straight out to a pawn shop in Bondi Junction and bought my first Super8 camera. So it was a sobering experience to be now pointing a camera at my film-making idol and the greatest contemporary London writer.

The Rotherhithe stretch was Kötting's memory ground from his days on the Pepys Estate in nearby Deptford and early jobs around the last days of the docks. 'The noise of memory', had plagued his walk with Sinclair, the soundscape worked into grooves in the tarmac by years of passage over the same terrain, the footsteps releasing voices like the needle on a turntable. They were in good form for the camera. We visited the Café Gallery Space in Southwark Park where they deposited found objects from the Thames shore as an impromptu installation. In Andrew's old favoured café on Lower Road, Surrey Quays he talked of how he was converted from lucrative odd jobs as a painter and decorator to the art world by film nights at the home of BBC Film Night presenter Philip Jenkinson. These screenings were referred to as 'straps' as Jenkinson would metaphorically strap the viewer to their seat while he ran flicks from his archive. Jenkinson had used this archive to great effect when he was given the job on The Old Grey Whistle Test of providing film clips to play over the tracks of bands who couldn't perform live in the studio, accidentally inventing the music video. His pairing of Mike Oldfield's Tubular Bells with black and white footage of skiers gliding across the mountain snow is a work of art in its own right. It was at these nights that Kötting discovered the work of Richard Lester and Bruce Lacey and before long was making his own avant garde films and presenting them at the London Film-Makers Co-op (another lost treasure of London).

Andrew and Iain talked of how their previous projects merged into each other, through the John Clare film By Our Selves, Swandown, and Edith Walks (which spawned the hypnotic The Whalebone Box). 'You have to beat the bounds', Andrew tells Iain wiping panini crumbs from his stubble, 'but the bounds are ever-changing and the bounds are morphing in and out of each other but you go back out there every day to try and find them again, it's

like you're scenting your territory, you're scenting the territory with words, with ideas, that always belong, but you don't know where they belong until two years later'.

Their tracing of John Clare's walk from Epping Forest to his childhood home in Northamptonshire saw Kötting make the journey in his film dressed as a Straw Bear, a character revived from rural folk custom. After dutifully following the railway to Queens Road, Peckham, our walk ended with Andrew stalking the Old Kent Road again garbed in the Straw Bear costume around the junction where he nearly died in a motorcycle crash just a year previously. It was a surreal and poignant end to a magical day.

One late January morning Iain and I met film-maker and noir novelist Chris Petit at Willesden Junction for a circuit of the area. In terms of the film, we were partly tracing the tracks laid down by the painter Leon Kossoff who had a studio nearby and produced a series of paintings of the railway sidings. But it was also the location of one of London's largest development plots, on Old Oak Common, one of Boris Johnson's 'Opportunity Areas'.

The plan was for a 'super hub' station that joined HS2, the line between London and Birmingham with Crossrail, and would be connected to Iain's 'Ginger Line' via a link from Kensal Rise station. The HS2 website claimed it would be 'the best-connected and largest new railway station ever built in the UK'. It's part of a wider scheme to build a Park Royal City on one of London's great industrial zones. On the day of our walk in 2016 the Evening Standard published a story announcing that a 'world famous cultural institution is to relocate to Old Oak Common in a breakthrough for Boris Johnson's plans to turn the desolate swathe of railway sidings and industrial estates into a thriving new west London district'. Just two months later in March, another Standard headline warned, 'Old Oak Common regeneration scheme risks being London's worst cock-up in 50 years'. The headlines since chronicle a series of failed schemes and thwarted bids, plans scaled back, homes cut and the word 'cock-up', begins to echo around the site. By the time London had gone into lockdown in March 2020 little progress had been made, apart from the demolition of a vacant hostel to make way for the building of the first new homes.

Willesden Junction is in fact located in Harlesden. A Saxon settlement, like Willesden and Neasden, the land that became the old London borough of Willesden had been given to the Dean and Chapter of St Paul's Cathedral by King Athelstan in 938 AD. Some of this gift had been passed on to All Souls College Oxford who owned the land around Kensal Rise and Kensal Green. 19th century maps show the giant Kensal Green Cemetery, beside the junction, marked as All Souls Cemetery. They are said to still own land in the area. The giant railway sidings were laid down across pasture and through pig farms. St Paul's had cleared Old Oak Common of its trees in the early 17th century. The Old Holt Wood of oaks and hawthorn recorded in the 16th century were simply recorded in the name.

Chris had lived in the area, Kilburn and Willesden Green. The main character in his cult film Radio On, one of the greatest English road movies ever made, is an in-house factory DJ inspired by the United Biscuits Radio Network feeding tunes to the workers in the United Biscuits factories across the land, including the large biscuit factory just along the Grand Union Canal in Harlesden. Chris was our local guide, navigating his own memory grounds.

Sinclair and Petit were collaborators of old, working on a series of films together for Channel 4 in the 1990s, the last of their kind to be broadcast on British TV. They chart a psychogeographical Sinclairian world of book dealers, marginal and not so marginal literary figures and cult authors, ex-gangsters, and edgeland landscapes. You could sense Iain and Chris's shared history as they plodded beside the railway tracks looking across at the wireless towers as we made our way to Harrow Road. 'Welcome to Harlesden' is spelt out in huge letters across the iron bridge, reminding you that despite the name this isn't technically Willesden (although in the old borough of Willesden). The traffic is brutal. I'm reminded of an essay by another great figure of British psychogeography, the filmmaker Patrick Keiller, who described a series of bicycle journeys along Harrow Road in search of locations to photograph around the time that Chris Petit was living in the area. One of the locations, northwest of Harlesden, became the subject of his first film Stonebridge Park, which includes shots of the same railway lines from a bridge over the North Circular less than two miles up the track.

As Iain pulled out the Leon Kossoff paintings to hold against the view from the bridge he said that this is 'a landscape of storage, transition ... it's the flood pool of the whole railway system'.

As we turned into Tubbs Road looking for Kossoff's studio, Chris was still tuning his sense of direction. 'I used to have this part of London burnt into my brain, I would struggle to get my bearings now'. Tubbs Road had been a shortcut to the North Circular, in a car not on foot, for escapes from the city. This appears to be a borderline of gentrification with multiple houses wrapped in scaffolding. Chris talked about how prices in this area had been climbing rapidly since the late 1970s, turning formerly working-class redoubts into celebrity hotspots. He mentioned how Peter O'Toole moved onto Mapesbury Estate a mile or two further north. Emma Thompson and Kenneth Branagh arrived back when they were the darlings of the British movie world. It was an improvement on the serial killer Denis Nilsen who'd committed some of his heinous crimes in nearby Melrose Avenue. The waves of gentrification had swept up from Notting Hill and Maida Vale in a pincer movement with a second front from Hampstead and Camden that swept aside Kensal Green and Rise, Willesden Green, Brondesbury and Queens

Park. And now the Old Oak Common Development Corporation was hoovering up the last of the industrial ground.

The sky was bleak and heavy as we made our way along Old Oak Lane, noting the proliferation of Portuguese cafes and other businesses that we'd passed in the area, making it redolent of another development zone at Vauxhall. Radio masts loomed over rows of railway cottages with 'Protect our Community' posters in pollution-stained windows. Endless traffic rattled and rasped down the road which we escaped by dropping to the towpath along the Grand Union Canal.

'The big change when I was in Kilburn was the development of Brent Park which was the first big Tesco superstore on the North Circular and also the first IKEA', Chris told us. Mid-'80's 'big shed' developments. The American Midwest arriving on London's northern fringe. Iain gazed across at the buildings lining the canal, presumably earmarked for deletion from the map at some point in the next decade. 'These strange brick cathedrals of vagrancy are much more in the mood of Asylum which you see as incubation cubicles for strange dreams', referencing one of their '90s filmic collaborations.

We were walking beside a development area which Iain said had come on a lot since he was writing London Overground, when it was just flat cleared ground. Now the site was marked by mounds of moved earth, shipping container site offices. In the following years it would spawn the Elizabeth Line depot. Iain sees parallels with the Lea Valley development and the freight that passes through Stratford, the canal and railway scoring the ground.

It felt as if my journeys were continuously connecting, impossible to escape the ripples of change oscillating out from Stratford. Even when I went mound hunting in the upper Lea, the threads still led me back to where I'd begun in the Olympic zone. I left Iain and Chris back on the Harrow Road after passing through St

Mary's cemetery, looking out for echoes of the cycling Keiller. We discussed the recently deceased David Bowie who'd generously allowed Chris to use the German language version of Heroes for Radio On, before I jumped back on the Ginger Line from Kensal Rise to Stratford.

It seemed appropriate then that the final shoot of the film was an evening spent in the Olympic Park alone filming Overground trains sliding through Brave New Stratford from as many angles as possible. Iain had moved on to the next quest, always in motion, taking the temperature of the city. We continue to walk together a couple of times a year, me always documenting with my camera.

I reframed the shot of the railway from the bridge beside the Aquatics Centre looking south through skeleton buildings that had been in embryo form for over a year. Then further north looking back along a cutting with the Westfield development and its offspring behind.

I got down almost trackside amongst tall stems of grasses and wildflowers. You had to give the planners credit for getting the planting right. Here the trains come quickly through the cow parsley and under a bridge. I shot the same Lea crossing side on, framed by the Olympic Stadium and the Orbital sculpture (surely not a cryptic tribute to Iain Sinclair's London Orbital?). This seemed like the last shot – I was happy with what I had – finally a wrap: with the East End Film Festival premiere nine days away it was mad to still be out there filming. Iain on several occasions referenced the 'Stratford hub' as the generator of the new London thrown up by the Overground even though it lies outside the circuit he walked twice with Andrew Kötting. And of course, it was integral to my study. Iain was escaping this 'over-narrated landscape', but I felt I had no choice but to keep returning.

CHAPTER 11

THE OPEN CITY

O ne of the outcomes of the London Overground film was that a team working out of New York University commissioned me to shoot some scenes for a documentary they were producing for the United Nations Habitat III conference taking place in Quito, Ecuador. The briefing document stated that they wanted shots of 'marketplaces, transportation, construction, and people going about their daily lives … the interactions between formal and informal commercial activity'. They particularly wanted me to visit Peckham Rye Lane. There was a certain irony to this in that Peckham Rye was one of the handful of the 35 Overground stops that we missed out of the film. Now the United Nations was sending me to Peckham.

I was greeted at Peckham Rye station by Jenny's Café in the station arcade with its abundant menu of all day breakfasts (Olympic Breakfast – two grilled eggs, three sausages, sliced tomato, beans and mushrooms – £4.20), burgers, wraps and toasties. But I was aware that I was on a mission for the United Nations so headed straight out to the main centre of interest.

Rye Lane had been the subject of an ethnographic study by a group of researchers from the London School of Economics. Their report had inspired the UN to despatch me south to capture these examples of 'interactions between formal and informal commercial activity'. The LSE study noted that Rye Lane was 'an intensely active retail strip' where 'the socio-spatial "scapes"... span local and global realities'. As I set up my tripod outside Jenny's I was struck by the similarity of this commission to the brief given to the character Robinson in Patrick Keiller's seminal 1997 film Robinson in Space. Keiller's unseen protagonist is commissioned by a 'well-known international advertising agency', who had heard of his study of London, 'to undertake a peripatetic study of the problem of England'. The film consists of static shots of facets of the industrial landscape of Britain in the mid-'90s, much like the tripod-mounted footage that I planned to capture of Peckham and a bunch of other locations I'd selected. Following this project, Robinson ends up spending time in prison and upon his release works for 'a network of non-human intelligences' in their determination to 'preserve the possibility of life's survival on the planet'. He then disappears without a trace leaving behind his canisters of film and notebooks in a derelict caravan in the corner of a field. However romantic this may sound, I hoped for a better outcome for my work.

Rye Lane runs through the site of the original Saxon village. 'The name of Rye given to Peckham signifies a common or an untilled ground', wrote Harold P Clunn in The Face of London (1932). In 1947 Clunn was to record that 'Many houses have been destroyed in Rye Lane and its tributary streets and also on the east side of Peckham Rye Common and in East Dulwich Road in successive air raids. No other part of London, except Croydon, has suffered more severely from the ravages of Hitler's flying and rocket bombs.' At the time the railway came in 1865, the area had been noted for its market gardens for a number of centuries. In 1630 Sir

T Gardyner, who occupied a manor located at one end of Rye Lane, mentioned in a letter to Lord Dorchester that his time was 'much occupied with growing melons and other fruits'.

Although the railway led to the development of Rye Lane as a shopping centre for the new commuters, a nursery was still evident opposite the station on the 1871 Ordnance Survey map.

A glorious art deco building stands on the ground adjacent to where the nursery was located, in the space between two elevated railway lines that curve around its elegant form. Now home to a Pentecostal church – part of an 'art deco quarter' – this single building almost fulfils the United Nations brief on its own. Built in the 1930s as a department store, later becoming a branch of C&A until the 1980s and now occupied by various businesses, a church and independent shops. An abundant fruit and veg stall ran along the side of the railway bridge, stacked with boxes of melons and green bananas, plantains, piles of yams, tomatoes, pumpkins, and tropical fruit I couldn't identify. Afro Foods stands next to a Cash and Carry. A pavement sign advertises 'Asian Take Away – Tandoori, Kebab, Fresh Nan'. A fella had set up a stall selling handbags and suitcases outside McDonald's. Fluorescent £5 signs clamped to torsos modelling brightly printed dresses flapped in the breeze next to a wig shop. An old lady loaded bags into her shopping trolley, a lanky cyclist pushed his bike along the pavement, double-deckers thrummed along Rye Lane in both directions. A spectrum of 'local and global realities'.

The Romans carved new roads across this ground connecting Londinium to the coast. More fanciful legends place Boudicca's last stand at the end of the road on Peckham Rye where William Blake saw angels. Sharp-eyed estate agents had visions of Rye Lane as the centre of another of London's 'coolest neighbourhoods', a 'New Notting Hill / Dalston / Brixton'. Its position has been so consolidated that Forest Gate was recently dubbed the 'New Peckham'.

A narrow indoor market branches off the main street, a hive of small traders and craftspeople. A fella bagging up a mound of dried Medina herbs beckoned me into his kiosk by telling me I looked like Karl Marx. Once inside he pulled out a copy of Mao's Little Red Book and raised a fist in salute. He told me he's been reading it since he was 12 or 14 years old and Mao has followed him on his travels from England to Jamaica and back again. The herbs, made into a tea, help deal with inflammation. I regret not buying a bag.

The Victorian and Edwardian high street has persisted through the Blitz and the shifting tides of commerce. Carved and moulded friezes, some freshly painted, adorn windows above the cosmetics shops and banks. Turrets stand proud in the face of Primark and Paddy Power. The Bussey Building is a multiple survivor. Originally built as a museum of firearms and gunnery it burnt down and was then rebuilt as a firing range and gun factory. Now it's a multi-use arts hub, co-working space, and club with a rooftop cinema. The Taco Queen resides near a Yoga Studio. A lady with pink hair and yellow stockings exited past my camera. The 363 bus lumbered past to Crystal Palace.

Holdron's Department Store, one of the crown jewels of Rye Lane, contains Holdron's Arcade, the kind of place haunted by contemporary surrealists and social theorists. The Parisian Arcades inspired poets and flâneurs. It's uncertain what will emerge from the Rye Lane Arcades. Holdron's imposing modernist hulk still loomed majestically over passing shoppers even though its glory days are long gone. It only merited a single mention in the 42-page local authority Conservation Area Appraisal of Rye Lane, and that's only to remark upon its survival.

Content that I'd documented enough 'interactions between formal and informal commercial activity' in Rye Lane I decamped to Jenny's to sample one of the all day breakfasts. Sat over my ironically chosen Early Starter breakfast (scrambled egg, slice of toast, tomato, a rasher of bacon, beans and two hash browns) I contemplated what I'd captured, wondering whether it matched the expectations of the filmmakers in New York laid down by the LSE ethnographic study of Rye Lane. There was the vibrancy of the street scene around Rye Lane, the herb man quoting Mao, and the impression that the much-lauded gentrification was confined to an outpost in the Bussey Building. The real action for me was not around the Yoga Studio but in the covered markets and the arcades, draped in colourful fabrics dowsed in the swirling sounds from music kiosks. This would have come as no surprise to Walter Benjamin. The German sociologist dedicated the last thirteen years of his life up to 1940 to working on a 1073-page opus inspired by the 19th century Parisian arcades. Benjamin wrote that the arcade was a place where 'the Surrealists unearthed the City's unconscious'. The ultimate figure in the crowded arcades was the flâneur, for him epitomised by Baudelaire, engaged in 'aimless strolling, the ability to lose oneself in the crowd, populating one's solitude'.

The figure of the flâneur makes an appearance in the work of one of the authors of the UN report that my Peckham footage would help illustrate. Another celebrated sociologist, Richard Sennett writes of the flâneur 'walking the city to know oneself, somehow'. From across the page he managed to address my ruminations: 'An ethnographer studies others; a flâneur searches for self in others'. Was that why I was more drawn to the arcades? And did it also help explain my constant wandering of the city and its hinterland?

Presenting the finished film at the London School of Economics a few months later, Sennett explained the idea of the Open City that had been developed for the United Nations conference in Quito in collaboration with Saskia Sassen and Ricky Burdett. 'The city is closed as far as capitalism is concerned and the point of this project is to open it up and to find another way of seeing the city.' This was in opposition to the notion of an urban realm of 'isolated blocks in a park' beloved of the hugely influential modernist architect Le Corbusier. This also sounded like a pretty good description of East Village, a series of isolated blocks in the Olympic Park. This was one of the reasons I'd returned to Stratford to shoot landscape

scenes for the Open City film. Within one frame you could capture freight trains passing through from the new container port on the Thames sliding between freshly minted blocks of apartments sold on the international property market. This contrasted radically with the informal economic activity of Rye Lane. Mega City Stratford was breaking free of the boundaries of the Olympic Park and starting to maraud through the neighbouring lands. I took my camera down to see what was occurring around Hackney Wick and capture the continued Stratford development for the UN film.

'A major new office for Transport for London' was going up in the International Quarter, a project being delivered by Lend Lease, developers of the highly controversial 'regeneration' of the Heygate Estate in Elephant and Castle. I filmed cranes hoisting giant chains and men like Lego figures riding cherry pickers and hanging on the railings of the bare frame of the building. There was a great desert of dried earth cleared on the other side of the railway tracks, more new zones coming off the masterplan into reality. A DLR train overtook a convoy of freight wagons beneath a mountain range of dirt. From some angles all you see are construction sites – half-built towers, cranes, men in fluorescent jackets and hard hats – it's as if they're building it all from scratch again. Was this the Olympic legacy – a never-ending construction site?

A new city at Stratford built around a shopping mall was always on the cards even without the running and jumping. At the turn of the millennium, Naomi Klein wrote in her hugely influential book No Logo about the trend of 'branded towns', corporate-built private developments. She quoted advisor to the top media conglomerates Michael J Wolf observing that 'Maybe the next step in this evolution is to put housing next to the stores and megaplexes and call it a small town. People living, working, shopping, and consuming entertainment in one place. What a concept.' Stratford took this concept to a whole new level, not content with being a 'small town' it declares itself a 'City'.

More freight hammered the track on the way to London Gateway. Wild flowers shook and rattled in the wind. There was a shift in ambience around Here East, the innovation hub occupying the Media and Broadcast Centre built for the Olympics. It has its own branded shuttle bus from the station to this campus aimed at 'innovators, disruptors, visionaries'. Coffee-sipping delegations scooted past in a convoy of golf buggies. Across the still strip of water in Hackney Wick 19th century innovators, disruptors and visionaries invented plastic in a building no more than an Olympic sprint away, intended as a waterproof coating for tarpaulin. It was where a by-product of oil was first called 'petroleum', and some genius got the idea to put perforations in toilet roll. The impressive roster of 21st century disruptors have a lot to live up to.

Landscaped swaying grasses recalled its past life as Arena Field. Hackney Wick Stadium occupied part of the site. Built in the early 1930s with a reported capacity of up to 50,000, Hackney Wick Stadium led a colourful life hosting greyhound racing and speedway right up to its closure in 1997, etching itself into the folklore of the area. Commenters on my YouTube videos told of a dodgy nightclub under the stands called Cherry's. Friday night Speedway with Dads, 'Make it a date Friday night at Eight'. There were also memories of a Second World War army camp at Bully Fen where post-war the ground was strewn with 'old steel helmets and gas masks'. Another dubious nightclub was located in nearby Eton Manor on Temple Mills Lane called the Spooky Lady in the White Hart pub: it later became a nightclub called the Flamingo. The White Hart can be seen on the 1902 map beside the Lead Mill Stream (elsewhere called the Waterworks River) at the top of Bully Fen. Mouxbar, a regular viewer, wrote about 'Raving to the early hours in seemingly the middle of nowhere (as far as London goes). Very odd place, essentially a Victorian / Edwardian pub with the rear wall knocked through into an industrial unit. The metal sides used to rattle to the music.' Graham remembered the legendary Eddy Merckx winning a televised cycling special at the Eastway track in 1977 'by a tyre width'. Such a different world from what stands on the same ground now.

A pair of swans glided along the Hackney Cut. The old canal-side buildings stared back at Brave New Stratford from across the water. I crossed the bridge beside the Eton Mission Rowing Club, a survivor of the former life, into Wallis Road. A large mural by street artist Noir adorned the side of an industrial building that had until recently been the home of Shapes nightclub. 'RIP London Clublife', was written on the wall. Shapes had been unable to re-new its entertainment licence, its closure seen as part of a trend forcing the more irregular nightspots out of East London looking for homes further afield, with some club promoters decamping as far afield as Berlin in search of a less hostile regulatory regime.

Aside from the ground-breaking developments in chemical engineering, Hackney Wick was famous for its sweets. Clarnico Confectionary was a dominant force in the area from 1870, famous for its mint creams. The building where plastic was invented was covered in graffiti: BRK KEV – whatever that means. The Lord Napier pub was buried beneath layers of coloured paint, 'From Shithouse to Penthouse' written along its length in large script. 'Aint Nothing Going Up But the Rent.' 'Meanwhile in East London Lunatics Decorate a Building...'

A friend from northwest London, Ian Long, told me about his family who lived in White Post Lane. The Lord Napier was their local before the war, his grandfather's horse and cart was trained to stop at the pub and intuitively knew when he'd had enough and it was time to carry him the short distance home. He passed along stories of shell-shocked First World War soldiers living rough on the marshes earning a few coins as 'look-outs for illegal gambling dens'. One of them went by the name of Poofer Ood. The rubber factory where Ian's great-uncle worked was apparent-ly known for causing brain damage to its workers. Fortunately, his relative's work kept him outside and he lived to a ripe old age, brain intact.

Shellac was also manufactured in the area, pressed into those old 78s and 45s. You can imagine how it must have smelt with all the chemical works and refineries. A fella called Anthony told me how when the wind whipped up it carried the odours from W Curley & Sons' Fat and Bone Merchants who rendered down butchers' waste for soap. Now the pong carried on the breeze was from the artisan coffee roasters near Carpenters Road.

A woman threw metal strips down from an upper floor window of Central Books warehouse into a skip. A sign on the door said they'd moved to Dagenham – a key component of the London book trade forced out to the fringe. A plaque marks the memory: Lesney Matchbox Toys – closed in 1982. It's like walking through a curious museum of the industrial past. These changes were predicted in the London Plan of 1944 that sought to protect the Lea Valley from over-industrialisation caused by the relocation of factories out of the East End to the Lea Navigation and Stratford railway hub. What was proposed was the creation of a 'continuous green wedge' linking East London to the Hertfordshire countryside. Quite how the residential and retail developments around the lower Lea Valley fit into this plan in the 21st century is unclear. But at least the air smells sweeter.

Hackney Wick was a building site, Fish Island invaded by an army in hard hats and orange vests. Cement mixers moved through the ruins like Tiger Tanks.

I captured the rhythm of construction on my camera, the swaying hoist arms reaching up from scaffolding swathed in plastic netting to land the catch of precious building materials. The music of hammered steel and engine noise, voices raised over the din to call out instructions. Another layer of the palimpsest is coated over the past and beneath it all, the marsh mud stirs. The spirits of place that have seen it all from prehistoric swamp through humans crouched by the wide riverbanks when water covered all of this land, and through the Romans laying their road across the Old Ford to the Danes sailing up to Hertford. And those genii locorum will see the days when these apartment blocks are nothing but blank blocks on an antiquated map.

The walk around Hackney Wick was narrated by the graffiti on the walls: 'Optimus Prime Minister'. 'Dead Bodies and Shopping Trollies.' 'Broken Homes' painted in big letters on an old brick canalside building. 'Just Lost the Game.' 'Dinosaur's Dying Wish.' There wasn't a lot of optimism evident in the graffiti and you could see why. 'Hashtag Save Hackney Wick's Artists.' 'Save Vittoria Wharf.' The artists making a valiant last stand at Vittoria Wharf had gone before I could answer their call for help.

There was a huge vacant plot next to the Hertford Union Canal awaiting a plan. An apartment development spawned from the site of a former furniture factory at Carpenters Wharf. At Swan Wharf blocks of flats are marketed with selected highlights of the heritage of the area. The view back towards Stratford from White Post Lane of the futuristic block the contrast is extreme – a whole other city. The area of London that made the future has become the past that is no longer wanted. The river once again a border like it was in the Dane Law. There is evidence of Ricky Burdett's claim that one of the successes of the Olympic Park development is that it has opened up an East-West passage as commuting cyclists zipped past in numbers.

The erasure of the names feels unnecessary: Eton Manor and Bully Fen, the Pudding Mill Stream and High Meads are gone, yet Chobham Farm is retained. The swaying grasses beside the Hackney Cut recall that wilder past etched in black and white on the 1867 OS map. Aside from a reservoir just to the north of where I stood on the east bank of the Cut the only building nearby was the cottage at Old Ford Lock and Nobshill Mill. Then there was the expanse of marshes to the north only broken by Temple Mills.

The development is endless, stretching along Stratford High Street and beyond down through Sugar House Lane and London City Island all the way to the Thames. It then sweeps around the Royal Docks. A hoarding on Albert Island proclaimed that 'London is Moving East'.

At the start of these journeys I saw the Lea as the barometer of change across London. As I've walked around the city I've seen the same pattern of development elsewhere. The pulverised remains of the Nestle factory at Hayes, development at Brentford, Northolt, Wembley, Nine Elms, Woolwich, Greenwich, Thamesmead, Lewisham, Barking, Edmonton, Elephant and Castle. Since my walk around East Village in the first post-Olympic Summer, the former Athletes' Village has started to become a place with its own stories. People have approached me to say how much they enjoyed living there. I heard about how it's entering new phases of life and original residents grumble at more recent changes.

I returned for a stroll around the Olympic Park in May 2020 during the Coronavirus lockdown. Cycling families streamed over the bridge from the Eastway past the Velodrome. People sat reading, half-hidden in the mature planting, hiding from the anxiety of the pandemic. It felt like a refuge from the madness of the time. The never-ending construction held in suspension. The new 'villages' of East Wick and Sweetwater frozen in an embryo state. The Stratford Waterfront Development, or 'East Bank', a field of cranes where the BBC, V&A, Smithsonian, and Sadler's Wells will spawn offshoots. I realised that I had finally come to terms with it. The questions of ownership, the displacement and replacement of people, industries, and wildlife were still there, the enquiries would be ongoing – part of the ever-evolving narrative of change. This zone of disruption that had sparked an odyssey that had consumed the best part of nine years had been accommodated into my personal psychogeography of the city. The casual flouting of lockdown rules by the groups of lads clustered around park benches, the people playing football and frisbee and having picnics a sign that it was becoming part of the Open City.

Stood on an artificial hill crowned by the Olympic rings, I remembered a bizarre evening near the start of this journey. I'd been invited to a gathering on the rooftop of the Balfron Tower in Poplar, a couple of miles south along the Lea. A group of people sat in a circle in a 24th floor apartment in this Brutalist masterpiece that had been at the centre of a controversial regeneration that saw its council tenants decanted and the flats sold off. They were urban planners, architects, academics, regeneration specialists, and somehow me. It was the day that Boris Johnson, then Mayor of London, had announced the plans for a cultural quarter in the Olympic Park, with the clumsy title of 'Olympicopolis' (you can see why they finally went with East Bank). An influential voice on London development spoke loudly to the group lauding the announcement and denouncing opposition. They used to say London moved East a mile every ten years, he declared, now it's more like a mile a year. It made you wonder where he thought Poplar was if it wasn't already in London till the money from the West had forced out its residents. Looking across the scene from that hill, that prediction seemed to have been borne out.

I realise now that this story will not have a tidy ending. The journeys and encounters are never-ending in a city like London. In my self-appointed role as one of the capital's many chroniclers and documenters, I understand that I must continuously stalk the streets making notes, taking pictures, shooting videos, and asking questions.

ACKNOWLEDGEMENTS AND THANKS

Peter Urpeth for his wise editorial guidance and support. Peter's morale-boosting feedback on the manuscript was essential for getting this book into print. David Osmond for his brilliant and patient proof-reading. Stephen McNeilly for doing such a fantastic job typesetting the manuscript. Patrick Knowles not only for his amazing cover design but also for advising me on the publishing process. Without their support you wouldn't be holding this book in your hands. A huge thank you must go to all the amazing people I met during the events covered in this book. Iain Sinclair for being a constant inspiration, for the walks, and the quiet encouragement. Dave Binns and Gary Lammin for leading me back out into the forest. Dan Clapton at The Wanstead Tap and Vivian Archer at Newham Bookshop for all their support over the last ten years and hopefully many more collaborations ahead. To my viewers on YouTube who've constantly reminded me to stay on track with publication, and my wonderful supporters on Patreon. Finally, my amazing wife Heidi for her endless support, love and patience.

Milton Keynes UK
Ingram Content Group UK Ltd.
UKHW040718161023
430697UK00001B/5